THE COUNTRYMAN'S
BEDSIDE BOOK

The Wayside Fire

THE COUNTRYMAN'S BEDSIDE BOOK

by
'BB'

Illustrated by
D. J. Watkins-Pitchford

MERLIN UNWIN BOOKS
LUDLOW, ENGLAND

First published by Eyre & Spottiswoode Ltd (October, 1941)
This edition published by Merlin Unwin Books (2006)

ISBN 1 873674 94 5
ISBN 978 1873674 94 9

Published by:

Merlin Unwin Books
Palmers' House
7 Corve Street
Ludlow
Shropshire SY8 1DB (U.K.)

www.merlinunwin.co.uk

British Library Cataloguing-in-Publication Data:
A catalogue record for this book is available from the British
Library

Printed in Great Britain by Biddles Ltd, King's Lynn.

To
IDA MARY DOWNING

'The wonder of the world, the beauty and the
power, the shapes of things, their colours,
lights and shades; these I saw. Look ye also
while life lasts.'

Introduction

This book has been written from an accumulation of notes which I have made over a number of years and contains all kinds of odd happenings and incidents of sport and natural history. In some cases it may simply be the description of a scene or an effect of colour, of a walk or a wood, a field pond or a hedgerow. It is perhaps more in the nature of a scrap book in which I have recorded all those things which interested me in my rambles afield.

Bearing this in mind perhaps the reader will not become too impatient when I skip from one subject to another like a field cricket in the sun.

This book was begun long ago in the days of peace and is concluded in the darkest hour in our history. I believe that because men have been so blind to nature and followed their own ideals we now find ourselves in this gloomy place. Could we but realize that it is the simple and natural things that matter, we should find the way to the perfect life. It is the artificial world of our own creating which employs most of our energies and interests, yet how pathetically we long for peace and quietness and the loveliness of this green island of ours. Greed and jealousy and all the baser human attributes seem to have gained the upper hand. Our life is brief enough in all truth yet, like spoilt children, we cut it short.

In the present century there has been a sudden awakening to the beauty of natural things; the old philosophers took them for granted, so much so that they never even wrote about them. Now we are beginning to realize what

Nature means to us and how, inwardly, it is part of ourselves and we of it. Is it too late?

One day this dark dream will be over, the iron of winter will pass, the village bells ring out again over the tranquil meadows and we shall have peace again. When that hour comes let us help to build a saner, simpler world on the one true foundation.

Nature is master of all, there will be wild violets blooming along the sheltered bank whatever we may do, the joyous birds will sing, grass will cover the old scars. In this I find quiet comfort and a pointer to Man's folly.

'BB'

NORTHANTS, *April* 1941

Contents

Contents

List of Illustrations

FULL PAGE PLATES

HEAD PIECES

List of Illustrations

INSETS

TAILPIECES

THE OLD UNHAPPY THINGS

Clean pebbles spotted like a trout,
Where ripple patterns meet,
Wild Iris blades, and in and out
The prints of secret feet,
Green catkins hanging in the rain,
The easy grace of wings;
Time to forget, time to forget,
The old unhappy things.

A willow set with silver studs,
Wry mirror of the stream,
Prim pattern of a folded bud,
The hawthorn's ivory dream,
In quiet woods where no man comes
A mottled song thrush sings,
'Time to forget, time to forget',
The old unhappy things.

1941

CHAPTER I

Cornish Road

Chapter I

W. H. Hudson describes the habit of jotting down notes as 'gathering sticks'. This is a good simile, for in time one finds there are enough to make a fire,—or a book, according to the mood of the moment.

This custom of carrying a notebook on various journeyings is one I have followed for a number of years, for only by putting down on paper one's immediate thoughts and reactions can one hope to preserve a faithful picture.

I like to think of Hudson wandering over the downs which attracted him so strongly, talking with the shepherds and watching the clouds go over, observing with minute care every bird, every incident which came to him. And then, after a long day spent in the open air, returning to his lodgings in some remote village to write down what he had seen.

Most of these incidents are very ordinary in themselves yet Hudson could see them in a new way, from a different angle, and through his simple and powerful prose they take on a magic we should have missed.

This I think is the chief charm of his writing; when we read his books we suddenly become aware that we too have

3

seen just that same incident—such as the floating thistle-down described in *Nature in Downland*—yet were blind to the inward beauty of the passing hour.

And as at the moment my thoughts are turning to Hudson I must relate a curious coincidence which happened to me recently.

My wife and I were visiting Cornwall for the first time, gathering material for a book on Cornish birds by the late Dr. Walmsley, entitled *Winged Company*.

One evening we found ourselves on the road from St. Ives to Zennor. About a mile out of St. Ives we saw a stockily built man walking along the road in front of us. He turned about as we approached and as he seemed to be wanting a lift we stopped and offered to help him on his way.

It turned out he was like myself, an artist, one John Barclay who lived in a little cottage in which D. H. Lawrence spent a good deal of his Cornish life.

As my particular study was birds he was able to tell me a good deal of interesting things about the local species and incidentally of the finest scenery.

He told me that within a mile or two of his cottage there was a buzzard's nest, built in the cliff-face of a lonely cove.

As he talked my eyes were on the dark moorland spread out below us, the patchwork of the fields, the innumerable banks and scattered farms, all small and grey and just a little mean. It was an evening of golden light. The black-thorn was in full bloom, not so white as the Devon black-thorn, but speckled sparse and grey on the low crouching thickets.

The distant edge of the cliffs was dark under a brooding sunset cloud and even though it was almost summer there was a strange sense of desolation in the scene before us. The road wound away round the shoulder of a moor, against the misty gold of the sunset strange rocks were stacked. Some-where to the right, in the fearful cliffs which fell hundreds of feet to the sea, the buzzard had its nest.

I went the next day to find it. About the squat grey farms the first swallows were hawking and from every blackthorn thicket came the lilting song of the chiff-chaff. After crossing a deep and noisy stream which tumbled its way joyfully to the sea I came to a cove. When I topped the ridge of the next hill the confused roar of the Atlantic surf loudened and through the booming cannonade came the thin mourning cries of gulls.

Barclay had given me a rough idea where the nest was built but it was some little while before I found it. After scrambling about for some time I came to a deep chasm where the sea had bitten into the granite cliffs, an awesome place.

A buzzard flew out from under my feet, so judging the nest to be in the cliff face below me, I crossed the head of the chasm to get a view of the rocks through my glasses. When I got to the other side however, no nest was to be seen though I scanned every ledge and cranny. I gave it up as a bad job and went back to the other side. Almost immediately the hen flew off a ledge directly opposite me and flapped, mewing, away, to perch on a distant rock pinnacle. My glasses picked out the nest which was built on a narrow ledge about ten feet from the top of the cliff. It was a surprisingly slight affair, a mere scrape among the turf, with a few heather branches arranged round the edge of the nest. I could see three eggs, appearing from this distance no larger than wren's eggs.

Just above the nest was another, a bulky affair of sticks and roots, built under an overhanging cornice. Both appeared quite inaccessible, even with the aid of a rope. I lay down on the very lip of the chasm, behind a tuft of heather which I drew across my face, and waited for the hen to return but she would not do so. She sat on the top of a rock about a quarter of a mile distant, mewing occasionally and preening. Very soon her mate joined her and they sat side by side for over half an hour. Tired of waiting I returned to the road.

Very soon I met a farmer driving two horses, harnessed to a harrow, coming down the lane, and he stopped and talked to me. He told me an interesting thing about the buzzards. They had nested in that particular chasm for as long as he could remember, and had always done so in his father's time, and for aught he knew long before that, for his family had lived in that farm for many generations. As a young man, he said, he had quarrelled with the buzzards for they had taken some of his tame pigeons. He was very fond of pigeons and the buzzards had taken them one by one until there were none left.

This surprised me for it is usually a comparatively cowardly bird, feeding on voles and young rabbits, grass-hoppers, and other insects caught among the grasses and whins on the tops of the cliffs. But the buzzards were so wary that he could not get a shot at them and after a while he had left them alone, and they were now friends again.

Suddenly he asked me whether I had read any of Hudson's books? When I said 'yes', he asked me if I had read *The Land's End*.

Now as it happened, I had never read it, but only that morning in Newlyn, I had seen that very book in a shop window and had bought it. Then it appeared the farmer knew Hudson and remembered him well, a tall bearded man with keen black eyes. He had come to talk to the boys in the village school about birds and beasts and the farmer had very vivid memories of those dark piercing eyes, which he said, noticed things which other people passed by. One quarrel which the farmer had with the book was that Hudson makes out the farmers, as a class, to be uncouth and uneducated peasants, uncivilised folk who were little better than beasts.

If this farmer I was speaking to was typical of the Cornish farming class then Hudson must have been unjust, for this man was well educated and talked as intelligently, and a great deal more so, than many so called 'educated' people I have met.

Standing there in the strong evening sun, with his hands on his harrow-handles, he seemed a noble man with a dignity and ease of bearing. When I left him I carried away with me the curious sense that Hudson was still alive and his spirit walking with me across that sunlit cliff.

On reaching the Gurnard's Head Hotel I told my wife of the strange coincidence of the book *The Land's End*.

After supper something prompted me to go out again and I went alone, for the first time, down to the Gurnard's Head rock. The light was fading, away on the calm sea a magnificent sunset flamed, with cornices and stacks of cloud low down against the yellow glare, shaped fantastically like the very rocks before me.

I scrambled up the cliff and soon saw, placed on the highest pinnacle of rock, what I took to be a bird, with its head sunk in its shoulders. As I drew near however it did not move and I began to marvel that the rock could be so fashioned, it stood out so solid and black. Nearer and nearer I approached and then at last I saw it was indeed a bird, a female peregrine. She sat hunched on the rock within twenty yards of me, gently bobbing her head.

That picture will long remain with me; she seemed to be the very spirit of this primitive and cruel coast, brooding there against the dying sky, black, black as the rock itself that frowned towards the loud and darkling sea. At last she dropped off into space with a leisurely flicker of sickle wings and was gone.

I chose a flat rock which overlooked the sea and sunset and for a long while sat there watching the slow rounded Atlantic rollers mechanically marching in one behind the other to burst in a smother upon a reef at the foot of the cliff. Cormorants flew low above the surface of the heaving waves so that they threw a shadow upon the water and I saw noisy white gulls far down the cliff, ranging themselves for the night on a massive rock.

I cannot say that Hudson was in my mind at the moment, indeed I think I had forgotten all about him, and of my meeting with the farmer up the sunny stony road. There was so much to see spread out below. Each roller as it moved inexorably towards the cliff caught the sunset's flare on its rounded back and when they hit the rocks I could feel the cliff shudder at the impact. What power in those slow battering rams!

When I got back to the Inn I chanced to open the book, *The Land's End*, for the first time and I immediately saw these words:

'The rocky forelands I haunted were many but the favourite one was Gurnard's Head, situated about midway between St. Ives and Land's End. It is the grandest and one of the most marked features of that bold coast. Seen from a distance, from one point of view, the promontory suggests the figure of a Sphinx, the entire body lying out from the cliff, the waves washing over its huge black outstretched paws and beating on its breast, its stupendous deformed face composed of masses of granite looking out on the Atlantic. I was often there afterwards spending long hours sitting on the rocks of the great head and shoulders, watching the sea and the birds that live in it; and later when April set the tiny bell of the rock pipit tinkling, and the wheatear, hovering over the crags, dropped its brief delicious warble, and when the early delicate flowers touched the rocks and turf

Common Buzzard

with tender, brilliant colour, I was more enamoured than ever of my lonely castle by the sea.'

He goes on to speak of a vision he had upon the Gurnard's Head of a hunter who, wearying of his sport, went to sleep upon a jutting ledge of rock and fell into the sea.

Hudson awoke after his vision believing that he too was falling from the rock. He concludes:

'In a moment I became awake, for I did not wish to perish by accident just yet, and, jumping up, I stretched out my arms, stamped my feet, and rubbed my eyes vigourously to get rid of my drowziness; and then sat down quietly and resumed my watch of gulls and gannets.'

So that the rock on which I sat may have been the very rock where the great naturalist had his dream and watched the sea that summer day so long ago.

In another part of the book I also found references to the Inn where I was staying and a whole chapter on Zennor itself. And in my fancy I thought that maybe his spirit had been transformed into that black hunched figure of the peregrine which seemed so unafraid of my approach.

I had other talks with the farmer mentioned earlier in these notes and was able to catch a glimpse of what life means to a man in this part of the country who must battle with the grim and stony ground of Cornwall. He told me some interesting things about adders. They were common on the cliffs, especially in springtime, and the places to find them were stony hedges facing the sea (a hedge in Cornwall is a raised bank, sometimes surmounted by a wall) and he described how, one afternoon, as he and his brother were having their tea in a little meadow near the top of the cliff, they had a bad fright from an adder.

It was a very hot day, a Sunday, and they were sitting under one of these hedges in the full blaze of the sun. He put down his cup, full of tea, close beside him on the grass, and a minute or two later happened to glance towards it. There, within a few inches of the cup was a viper, weaving its head from side to side, about to strike at his hand!

He had lost several dogs through adder bites, one a very valuable spaniel. It was bitten in the throat and died in great agony. Sheep are very often bitten when grazing on the cliffs, usually through the nose.

He went on to talk of other things and as was perhaps natural, of wrecks. Many people will remember the tragic loss of the St. Ives lifeboat crew one wild winter's night a few years ago.

That night, he said, was the worst he had ever experienced, with the wind reaching a force of nearly a hundred miles an hour. So terrific was its strength nothing could stand up against it and when he went out to look at some calves he had in an outbuilding of the farm his lantern was repeatedly blown out. Even in the shelter of the stone walls of the yard he could scarcely stand. Next morning he had news of the loss of the St. Ives lifeboat crew who had gone out to answer a signal of distress farther down the coast, but where the wreck was no man knew.

It was not until next day, when the wind had abated and the sun shone once more, and the business of the farm could continue, that he saw wreckage in his cove. Eleven bodies were brought up out of the cruel sea, all stripped of their clothes, some torn and mutilated beyond description by the ferocity of the waves.

It was the very cove where I had found the buzzard's nest and when next I saw that lonely place, with the translucent sea, the colour of a zircon or some other rare stone, beating its sonorous rhythmic pulse among the black rocks, I thought of that wild night when the sea showed itself in its most terrible and merciless mood.

Lying on the warm turf among the soft cushions of the

thrift and the scent of the golden gorse (strongly reminiscent of some tropical fruit) I thought of this spirit of the sea as some god or evil thing that had killed so many of my kind.

If all the men, women, and children that the sea had claimed since man first walked the earth, were to rise out of the waves and come trooping up the white sand two hundred feet below me, they would number many millions, more than the eye could count.

Perhaps there is a spirit of all natural things which must be appeased from time to time by human sacrifice; a spirit of fire, disease, and now, in the present age of machinery, a new spirit who is insatiable and who claims so many thousands each year and every day.

Though my memories of Cornwall are sunny ones, of golden gorse and speckled blackthorn and enchanting green seas washing loudly among the caves, I have one memory of a great gale, almost as great a gale perhaps as that in which the lifeboat crew was lost.

It was the day after I found the buzzard's nest. Instead of the calm warm light of the low sun shining upon the crags, there were lowering clouds and driving hail which stung the face like thorns driven into the flesh. It was quite impossible to open one's eyes fully to watch the sea, and what a sea!

There is a place not far from Zennor called 'The Horse's Back'. It is a rib of rock which juts out from the mainland far into the Atlantic, forming a gully very like that in which I found the buzzard's nest, though if anything more awe inspiring. It is hardly wide enough to walk down the rib, though a daring climber could do so and think nothing of it.

That morning I stood, or rather crouched, on the sloping slippery cliff above and watched the huge rollers, walls of green translucent water, come surging up that narrow alley with mighty detonations, to break in driven white foam that was enhanced by the ebony rocks.

c   C.B.B.

Down in that frightful black abyss, where the rocks gleamed wet with spray, a gull was perched, a big handsome fellow, and every now and then, as though to cry defiance to the waves, he opened wide his mouth and let forth a hellish ringing laugh which I could hear above the noise of the surf.

Other gulls came sailing in over the chasm, tilting unconcernedly in the roaring gale, alighting on the ledges in the most blasé fashion. Wild weather is nothing to them, they glory in it. Different indeed from the poor little sand martins and swallows I had seen earlier in the day, flitting, like butterflies after a shower, in the lee of a bank by Marazion marsh. One little sand martin seemed utterly spent. It crouched on the wire of a fence rocking miserably to and fro, with its head sunk into its shoulders. Then I saw the whole corner of the pool alive with swallows and martins, hovering just above the surface of the water, evidently catching flies, though it was hard to believe any insect could live in such wild wind and wet.

What a rude welcome it must have been for those poor feathered sprites, newly in from across the sea.

Not far away, a shoveller drake all resplendent in his gorgeous plumage, was diving about in the shallow water, upending like a domestic duck to find succulent morsels in the weeds. Close to him was the duck, likewise engaged. Soon they saw me watching them and swam slowly away to a screen of slender reeds and were lost to view.

Before very long the weather changed, the wild wet clouds blew away from the moors and there began the loveliest summer we have had for many years.

I was speaking just now of The Horse's Back, near Zennor. The most impressive thing about this particular rock formation is the way the rollers, as they enter the narrow cleft or passage are piled up, and what a moment before was naked glistening rock is buried the next instant under many feet of swirling water. Then, at the shock of impact, the granite trembles, white foam shoots high in a graceful pillar to drift and melt magically away.

At the height of the storm I happened to glance upwards at a castellated battlement of jagged granite just in time to see two peregrines come curving over the edge, both in their element and revelling in the gale.

This brings me once more to the buzzard; I cannot leave him without relating a few more incidents with regard to this bird.

At first sight he seems noble, even royal as the eagle is royal, especially when he is seen sailing majestically on rigid wings above the crags and precipices.

Yet like some people one has met, on better acquaintance we find that he is in some ways a spurious bird.

Seen close at hand, the head is small and beak puny, and his feet, which one would suppose to be huge scaly talons with a gripping dagger-shod clutch, are undersized, barely powerful enough to hold an infant rabbit. He is also a coward and has none of the dash and ferocity of the falcon tribe.

I shall always carry in my mind a very lovely picture of buzzards. I was walking down a Devon lane one sunny morning in early spring. Primroses made gay yellow splashes on the rough steep banks of the lane where all manner of ferns were growing; hart's tongue, pennywort, and hundreds of other beautiful local ferns and plants which I never see in the prosaic midlands.

Not far away was a dense wood crowning a hill which overlooked the Dart, a wood in which trolls might conceivably dwell. It was composed of Corsican pines, a tree which thrives exceedingly in the rich red soil of Devon. Beneath the wood was a little flashing brook which wound its way down the green valley, in and out between groves of wild iris. Soon I saw a buzzard, sailing along beneath the wood, hardly moving its wide spotted wings. Its mate soon joined it and then they began a graceful spiral, still without moving

Buzzards in Devon

their wings, or appearing to do so, up and up, higher and higher as though they were swinging on invisible threads. Seen against the dark foliage of the pines they reminded me of two richly coloured moths.

Before long I heard, from high above, the thin mews of yet another buzzard and looking up I saw not one but three or four tiny specks against a huge white cumulus cloud which towered like a vast mountain against the soft blue of the sky.

The buzzards by the wood still continued their ascent, becoming smaller and smaller until they joined those other specks in the upper sky. It was wonderful to see the way the birds made use of every upward air current, tilting their fan-shaped tails and climbing round and round, higher and higher, until they also were mere dots high against the blue ceiling.

Not very far from the wood of Corsican pines there was an old quarry in the side of a hill. It was an interesting place and a paradise for birds.

Below the cliff of rock, which was the quarry's face, birch and alder grew thickly, the slender white stems of the former appearing as silver threads against the dark tones of the rock.

For many days I had heard a raven croaking and had often seen him winging his leisurely way across the valleys or tumbling in sheer ecstasy over the patchwork pattern of red and green fields.

I was sure the ravens had a nest in the quarry and when I explored the place I saw it, built on a ledge half way down the face of the cliff in a quite inaccessible position. It was a huge structure of twigs and sticks which had obviously been added to over a succession of years. I could not see whether it contained eggs, as the cup of the nest was too deep.

The raven turns up in curious places. I remember one hot afternoon in July in the old forest of Whittlebury hearing the deep croak of this kingly crow and seeing a pair fly over the trees. They may have been the descendants of ravens that had always lived in the forest since very early times. If it was not so persecuted the raven would be a common bird once more as it was in the days of Robin Hood.

Exhausted Sand Martin, Marazion Marsh

CHAPTER II

Cornish Cattle

Chapter II

The uttermost ends of Britain have something in common; a windswept wilderness, a treeless land, the same weather-worn farms which crouch, like the few stunted thorn brakes, with their backs, as it were, to the sea. But unlike Caithness, Cornwall has a gentler climate and consequently there is a limited tree growth in the sheltered places, twisted 'Arthur Rackhamish' blackthorn, heavy and bearded with grey green lichen speckled with greyish blossoms in the spring of the year.

These blackthorn jungles form magnificent cover for the numerous small warblers on their spring and autumn migrations. There is something rather strange in hearing the chiff-chaff's clear lilting song and the bubbling spring of the whitethroat in a country so devoid of real trees. One associates their song with the deep and leafy woods, among the branching ferns and forest glades where the foxglove and willowherb raise their slender spires.

I have often wondered why these stunted blackthorn thickets are so smothered with lichen. Is it some protection to the branches from the cutting sea winds?

The apple orchards of Devon are the same, but only the very old trees are covered. Down on the cliff tops the lichens are of a different order, some a bright rusty gold, a most rare colour which is a lovely contrast to the grey granite. I was reminded, in looking at these many coloured lichens, growing in flat 'seals' on the boulders, of the colour schemes of two of the greatest of the world's painters, Degas and Velasquez. Each artist was much in love with these soft harmonies, of grey and pink and gold.

Sometimes I have seen such a rock, smothered in gold and pink, against the green-blue of the sea below; then is the tonal and colour charm greater still.

As far as I remember, north of, say, Wick in Caithness there are no trees whatever, not even the stunted black-thorn one finds in Cornwall. Perhaps on those very northern hills the winds of winter are too fierce even for so hardy and iron-barked trees as the thorn.

I was amused the other day to see a Cornish farmer calling his cattle home on the cliffs by Gurnard's Head. The beasts were graceful, slender legged creatures, Guernseys, which I believe are more intelligent than the slow-moving brown and white cows of my native county, which seem more like big tanks in action.

The man stood by the gateway of the farm, clad in oil-skins from top to boot as though he were a sailor, and his long drawn cry was like the call of a sea bird on the cliffs.

A gale was blowing off the sea, rain-charged and stinging, and as the cows came into view each beast held its head at an angle to the wind and rain with eyes half closed, just as a man turns his face against driving sleet. They all came running in a line, as gracefully as deer.

These cliff top farms are always interesting places, especially in spring. Numberless rabbits live in the blackthorn thickets and among the gorse on the hillsides. Their young must form the staple diet of marauding buzzards. The slow worm is common along the stony warm banks of North Cornwall and the farmer mentioned in the preceding chapter had seen them many times.

The commonest bird of the cliffs, if we do not count the gulls and kittiwakes, is the jackdaw. There must be many millions all down the north Cornish coast. They wheel and fly in clamouring cohorts, swirling round the granite stacks, speeding like chimney smuts over the dizzy precipices, 'chakking' and talking to one another as they toss and turn.

Once at the Horse's Back I saw a wonderful picture of jackdaws. As I sat on the edge of the abyss a whole crowd of them, numbering about two hundred, suddenly came pouring over a rugged bastion of rock above my head and swooped with backswept wings in one long curved stream across the chasm.

That streak of speeding birds, forming such a graceful sinuous line which stretched, at one instant of time, from the uppermost rock to the far side of the Horse's Back made a grand wild picture, as though some cavern had opened in that upper pinnacle to release a crowd of black spirits which had been imprisoned there, away from the sunlight and the clear sea-laden air.

They hurled themselves down with such abandonment and joy, twirling and rushing and vanishing, as suddenly as they had arrived, over the ridge of the Horse's Back. I realized that never again would I, or any other, see such a spectacle, the same number of birds, the same light on the sea and cliffs, that same curling black thong, like the arc of a stock whip cutting across the sky, never again would that happen down the corridors of Time.

This knowledge made the experience even more precious. Do the same patterns in swirling water or in flame ever recur? I have often watched the ripples in the stream or the pattern of flame tongues in the fire and wondered if they are ever repeated. I doubt it, and in this way they resemble the stuff of which life is made.

All these cliffs on this part of the coast are adder haunted, especially on the lower heathery slopes.

It is strange to note the change and character of the cliffs as one moves farther north. Around Tintagel and Boscastle, indeed all down that northern coast, the good honest granite is replaced by treacherous slate.

Slate cliffs are ugly both in colour and form, and are not nearly so impressive to my eye as the rounded bastions and pillars of lichen-stained granite. There is no need to warn the rambler on the west Cornish coast of falling slate, the cliffs are well bound with thrift and short sweet grass. Around Tintagel there are notices everywhere warning those on the beaches to look out for trouble.

I went to Tintagel to search for the chough, a bird I have never seen in its wild state. But alas! I was disappointed. I scanned the cliffs in vain for a pair of cherry-red legs and a curved red beak, only innumerable jackdaws swung in smutty bugling companies about the ivy-festooned cliffs. I did however see a pair of ravens which flew low over my head, passing guttural remarks, the male bird tumbling as he flew. As the raven is re-establishing itself I hope that the chough will do the same. I do not share the opinion of other naturalists that the jackdaw is the sole cause of its gradual disappearance, there have always been thousands of jackdaws in the cliffs.

We do not know the cause of increasing scarcity amongst birds and animals of certain species. The case of the bittern and other birds of the fens, such as the night reeler and bearded tit, can be explained by the drainage and consequent lack of suitable food and cover, but there are other species which seem to have no cause for dying out; the kite

Spring in Devon

is one, and in the animal world, the red squirrel. Everyone knows that the kite was at one time a scavanger of London's streets, yet at the present time there are only a few breeding pairs left in Wales. As to the red squirrel I touch on this in a later chapter.

Inland Cornwall depresses me, as I suppose it does most people. I dislike saying unkind things about any county, but the numerous tin mines and patched up mean fences (every gap seems to have a rusty bedstead wedged across it, there must be enough old iron in Cornwall to build a fleet), the starved fields with their crumbling turf banks, weigh heavily on the spirit. Maybe it is the lack of trees which depresses me. I love trees, without them I am miserable, save in the down country, and even there one finds noble beech groves in the sheltered coombes. The deep grassy glade and rustling floor of woodland leaves enchants me. In Cornwall the only thing to break the monotony of the criss-cross walls and banks is an occasional tall chimney or a careless jumble of grey stone, not piled majestically as those Devon torrs, but a welter of shapeless stone, all higgledy piggledy anyhow.

There is something very Irish in some parts of the Cornish landscape, the same sense of man's weariness in battling with a stony and unkind ground.

And those mines! . . . Crossing the tussocky rock-strewn fields one stumbles on a ring of stones, often without a chimney near, and within the ring is a jungle of weeds and briars covering an old mine shaft, a gaping black mouth which gives back, after an awesome space of time, the rumbling echoes of a leaping stone. I think of those old deserted galleries and shafts (there must be many hundreds in west Cornwall) honeycombing the ground under one's feet, silent and dark as the furthermost pit, peopled maybe by the ghosts of the old tin miners, echoing to horrid ghostly songs and clank of buckets, full of the forgotten episodes and sounds of past times.

Round the weather-beaten crumbling chimney columns the wind pipes and moans, the trailing ivy creeper swings limply, jackdaws peer downwards at the intruder with their devilish pale eyes, eyes of insane imps; only the sky shows movement and colour and holds hope. It is a relief to get back to the granite cliffs and the thin wailing of white gulls, to the smell of the green seas battling and echoing in the numberless caves.

There is no softness in Cornwall, no prettiness or light gaiety, were it not for the cliffs and sea it would be a land accursed.

Out of the withered rush tussocks the drab pipits toss upwards, reeding their thin cheepings ; they seem to me to be the ghosts of miners' little children lost down the yawning shafts, and from the tumbled mess of yonder stone comes the evil harsh croak of a carrion crow, full of bitterness and cruelty.

The great winds come tearing in from off the sea, smiting the deformed thorn scrub that struggles for its life behind the tumbled wall. The branches scarcely whip about in the wind, they stand up rigidly as though made of iron against the force of the gale. Surely those timid sulphur sprites of migrating warblers must be glad to flee farther north to the gentle green coombes of Devon!

There is one friendly glowing thing in this land of grey and Rembrandtesque tones, and that is, in spring and early summer, the gorse. It is not such glorious gorse as one finds in Wales, the blooms are not so large or the bushes so big, but the flaming gold of its blossom cheers and even dazzles the sight. This dazzling effect is enhanced by the sudden contrast between rain sodden moorland, withered grass and heather and the flaming splendour of the full flowering bushes.

On a warm day on Zennor cliffs I have walked for a long way breathing in the delicious but slightly sickly scent of the acres of golden bloom.

There is a great fascination in sitting, or rather lying, on a springy mattress of heather at the lip of a cliff, watching the guillemots and gulls on the breeding ledges. The former sit row on row on the face of the cliff, many with tails outwards (these birds are usually asleep), while others sit facing the sea. All the time there is a coming and going. These little penguin-like creatures seem more like insects than birds, they remind me of bees round a hive.

One guillemot approaching the ledge spreads out its legs on either side of the tail at an angle of roughly 45 degrees, giving the impression of some sort of black insect with hanging legs.

Cornish Cliffs

At each fresh arrival other guillemots ranged along the cliff bob their heads and chatter at the newcomer, time and again turning their heads sideways to look about them.

It is very pretty in the breeding season to see the various love affairs going on beneath our eyes, and after a while one gets the idea that these little black and white people, so busy and important, are so very like ourselves.

Here on a ledge, the culminating act of courtship is being enacted, on another two sit close together caressing each other, while many hundreds of feet below two kittiwake males are engaged in what looks like a battle to the death on the surface of the sea. Locked in a close grip the birds flap desperately in circles, seemingly half drowned, worrying and biting, and rolling over and over in the water. They remind me of two gnats which have fallen into a pool and are endeavouring to rise again and fly away.

I could almost imagine some huge creature of the sea breaking water and engulfing the combatants as a trout gulps down a fly. But another passing gull swoops down and joins in, and all three fly away.

All the time, from the caves and crevices of the cliffs there rises up to the watcher among the heather and the sunlight a curious confused and musical murmur, very like a sort of tuneful humming in a hive or of a distant crowd all talking at once. There rises too, the smell of the guano mixed with the sea and numerous small flowering plants all around.

Far below, the hissing 'greenbacks' come creaming among the rocks and pebbles, swilling and sluicing the secret caves and crannies, sliding up the white sand of shadowed coves, retiring again to gather strength for a next assault. In the evening, when the humming on the ledges dies, the cliff bats come out and flicker round, diving and swooping about the frowning bastions like tattered scraps of burnt paper against the primrose sky. Past Zennor Head two wee fishing boats stand out bravely for the wide crinkled expanse of the calm sea, two sharp willow slips blown across a pond. Blacker grow the rocky forelands, the cowled monks on the Gurnard's Head bow forward to the sunset, eternally fixed and sombre, while away to the South'ard a wheeling loom of a lighthouse flickers round and is gone.

At such times these cruel cliffs and sombre land behind take on a softness and a calm. Out of sight and hearing of the sea, away back on the higher ground, little streams babble loudly in the quiet, and a yellowhammer, not yet abed, rings out his wild song from the top of a furze bush. In the furze too a few linnets remain awake, their twanging notes ravishingly sweet, their quick little heads turning this way and that, smiling eyes alert to danger from the sky.

It is a different Cornwall then, for evening brings a softness to all things and smooths away the hard lines. There is no thought of the grey winter winds, the whip of rain on the wet moor's face, the weary motor bus battling its way over the hills to the haven of St. Ives. There is no thought now for the Inn fire and drawn curtains, miry farm yards and dribbling gutters. For summer has come to the cliffs and moors, seals play over translucent green pavements of the shallower seas.

The Cornish streams are not so attractive as those of Devon, but near Zennor I saw a burn transformed into a very beautiful wild water-garden.

I was walking on the cliffs one day when a gentleman came up to me and offered to show me his garden. As water gardens are a particular weakness of mine I jumped at the chance and we went back along the cliff path to his beautiful house, overlooking a cove. Below its windows a broad stream came tumbling down the rocks. In the old days there had been a mill there but it had fallen into ruins these many years and the old mill pool had leaked and nothing remained but a few blocks of lichen-stained stone.

He had renewed the mill pool and rearranged the rocks so as to enhance the beauty of the water-falls. He was wise enough not to tame the stream and give it an artificial look, but had managed to preserve this true wild character, so that now in his garden, he could sit all day long and hear the water babbling past and watch it cascading over the rocks. Other small tributaries branched out from the main stream and at every turn of the path there were fresh delights, here a pool, crystal clear, under an overhanging mass of rock, here a miniature water wheel churning busily, in another place a swift running brooklet overhung with ferns and other wild flowers.

When he bought the place, he said, the stream was hidden under a jungle of bushes and rubbish and in many places it was simply a green bog. He had cleared its course, cut down and uprooted the bushes and had laid bare the stream in all its beauty. Looking at the way he had taken advantage of this wild stream and built his house so that its rush and glitter were for ever with him, I was reminded that so few humans ever do this; they build their houses, usually row on row, with no regard whatever to the natural surroundings. In some cases I have in mind, when there has been a stream, it has been fenced off and hidden from sight as though it were something to be ashamed of, and often when a rich man retires and builds himself a house he will select the most unimaginative site for it, some bare hill or other exposed place, and lay out the garden (or gets some other unimaginative person to plan it for him) in straight and angular lines, long paths neat and trim running at right angles to the house, and flower beds geometrically designed and planted with stiff and artificial flowers. If he plants trees they are the kind one finds in cemeteries, not the lovely wild trees such as birch and hawthorn.

If I could build my own house, before ever I had thought out the plan of it or the style, I should spend many days, perhaps years, seeking for the spot on which I should build it. There would have to be a stream and perhaps a pool and natural trees of all kinds. I should try to do what this man in Cornwall had done, and have before my windows the gushing stream so that its music would be with me always, winter and summer, spring and autumn, flashing bright in the sun of June or big with winter floods between the sodden banks. And like this man, I should build my house away from a town, perhaps even away from a village. It is not because I am an unsociable person, far from it, but always within the sight of trees and streams and earth unscarred by man's handiwork I should find what I most desire and which gives me the highest pleasure in life. The mind of man is, in the main, apparently incapable of appreciating the true loveliness which the earth has to offer. And it seems we are losing touch with nature, living in an artificial world as far removed from natural things as possible.

If there are grand old trees, cut them down, they will obscure the view, if there is a stream, hide it underground. Let us have, these people say, everything neat and trim, staring stucco walls, clipped hedges, sundials, yew peacocks, and ships, . . . away with nature, hide it up, it is untidy and untamed. Let us make the whole of England a suburban town, with rows and rows of houses all alike. The long straight pavement is far more useful than the mossy woodland walk with its dripping trees and mouldering autumn leaves; away with nature, away with it!

So it is that year by year England is becoming less lovely. The little gated lanes are going to be replaced by tar-mac roads and petrol pumps, and now the loathsome charabancs penetrate even the remote highlands.

It is but a phase, it will pass, one day these rows and rows of bungalows and houses will crumble and be covered by the old earth, trees will grow again, and the sweet clear stream burst from its prison and gush once more into the light of the glorious sun.

The hills and the downs may be scarred, and nature will, in time, heal the wounds.

The other day I was returning from the west country and

by the Wiltshire downs I saw a hideous example of what man can do. On the side of a lovely green down there had been cut, in letters many feet high, the slogan DRINK MORE MILK. What a brilliant example of the ingenious mind of man! Here was a magnificent advertisement perpetuated in the turf. Every time anyone chanced down that road (and it was a busy main road) they would see these letters, a natural hoarding. The chalk downs take long to heal, once scarred they show the blemish for centuries. The chances are that slogan will be there for hundreds of years, the larks will rise up and sing over it, and harebells nod in the sweet breeze. But by degrees the wild thyme, beloved of the bee, will cover the scars, grass will grow again and the ugly lettering will slowly fade, leaving only a slight depression in the close grained turf.

This is the quarrel I have with my own kind. Perhaps the root of all the evil is greed for gold, the greatest curse of mankind.

Close to my home there are the remains of two beech avenues. Only some two dozen trees are standing, though a few years ago these beech avenues were famed throughout the county for their beauty and stateliness.

I asked a native why the trees had been cut down.

'You will never guess', he said with a hint of pride in his voice, 'you will never guess what those trees were used for. They were made into ladies' shoe heels, yes, they were cut up and the wood was used for elegant high heels.' And I thought how strange it was that maybe at that very moment hundreds of women were walking about on an avenue of beech trees; trees that had known the gusty roar of wild winter gales; the delicate filigree of hoar frost when the bramblings and chaffinchs hunted for the sweet mast about their feet; a fairy mist of spring green which seems like heavenly rain when the sun shines through it. Trees that on the dark November days had held the fog between their arching branches, making the avenue a shadowed aisle loud with the drip of moisture.

I would a thousand times rather lay waste a whole street of houses than cut down such an avenue as this. In these days it takes only a few weeks to build a house but more than a generation to build a tree. One is a dead thing, the other alive, breathing with the earth and sky, even as we do.

Time can mature a house, colouring the stone work and staining the tiles.

In those Cotswold manors, dreaming amidst their bosky woods, nature has done much to soften and beautify man's handiwork, yet the loveliest house ever built by man is not more lovely than the beech in full maturity.

Fallen Beech

CHAPTER III

Stone Curlew in Flight

Chapter III

How wonderful it would be for a naturalist if he could go
back three hundred years and wander over the Wiltshire
downs in search of the great bustard. I have tramped many
miles across those chalk ranges in the hope of seeing the
next best thing, a stone curlew, which is really a small
brother of the great bustard, and when the latter bird was
found on the downs the stone curlew must have been his
constant companion.

There has always been something peculiarly appealing to
me in the thought of those huge turkey-like creatures
wandering about in droves. It is sad to think they are seen
no more; I can just picture a wide sweep of downland shim-
mering and quivering on a hot summer afternoon and far
away, moving slowly across the vast expanse, a herd of these
magnificent biscuit coloured and bewhiskered birds. In my
imagination, I can picture the bustard much more vividly
feeding on the downs of Wiltshire, than on the Norfolk or
Suffolk brecks; but it was common there also up to little
over two hundred years ago.

The stone curlew is still found in Wiltshire but only once
did I see him, or thought I saw him. I was riding, with

about fifteen other yeomanry, down a stony slope one boiling August day, when a bird which I took to be a stone curlew got up under my horse's hooves. The glimpse was such a fleeting one I could not be sure of identification and it was not until many years later that I had a clear view of this 'little bustard', as I prefer to call him, for the first time.

It was early May, I had gone down to Suffolk for a couple of days in the hope of seeing it, and the memory of my first view is vivid.

The weather was wonderful for early May, it might have been June; the vast rolling wilderness of flint speckled turf danced and jigged in the heat.

Away in the distance, crowning a downlike slope, was a long line of fir woods and about two miles off a shepherd was herding a flock of sheep. The turf underfoot was springy, not starred with harebell or thyme as on the Wiltshire downlands, but cushioned with grey lichen and tough tangled grass, withered yellow and matted closely so that the foot sank almost ankle deep in it. Here and there were sandy stretches with slight undulations, speckled all over with white and grey flints of all shapes and sizes and grown over in places with a close creeping mossy saxifrage of a dark red-brown colour. There were no flowers for it was still too early. A puff of breeze sent a spiral of sand sifting, veiling for the moment the distant line of dark firs.

As I walked across the stony plain, wheatears kept me company, the males in full breeding attire wonderfully spick and span in grey and black. They flirted from hillock to hillock bobbing their tails redstart fashion, their sand coloured breasts toning beautifully with the bare patches.

For many a weary mile I wandered on, seeing nothing but pipits, plovers, multitudes of larks, and a female sparrowhawk beating low over the breck.

And then a bird passed me half a mile away, flying like a

curlew with rather sharply pointed wings. I got my glasses on to it and saw immediately it was a stone curlew. The thick short neck and striking wing pattern was very prominent. The black and white bars on the wings show up from a considerable distance and soon identifies the species.

It pitched about a mile away among the flints and I began to walk across towards it, keeping my glasses at the ready and stopping ever and again to search the broken ground in front of me. At last it got up, seeming to appear as if by magic from the khaki tones of sand and turf. It was within fifty yards when it rose from a little sandy hollow and I had a good view, so clear that through the glasses I could see the round cat-like eye. I watched it wheel away with strong wing beats, one moment light against the distant wood, now dark against the sky. It first headed for a birch grove but a shepherd turned it and the last I saw of it was a faint blurred shape steering for a gap between two fir plantations.

Though I walked over to where it had disappeared I did not get another glimpse and I did not see it again that afternoon.

Late that evening however I went again to the breck. The burning sun had gone down in a crimson cloud beyond the dark line of fir woods, a sombre quiet had fallen on this strange wilderness of sand and flint. French partridges were calling and an occasional plover wailed. Then came the melancholy wild pipe that was unmistakable, a double note not unlike the cry of the common curlew but to my ear much more beautiful and haunting. It was a lovely scene; the dark sweep of the breck towards the sunset, a few wisps of rose coloured cloud low down in the west and this wild strange call coming to me in the quiet wilderness like an echo of bygone times. And very soon I heard others answering on the far side of the road. Then two dark shapes passed and I saw four stone curlew, all flying together. They wheeled about, calling one to another and finally flew past me within twenty yards, black against the sky. One lit on a sandy bluff and I walked towards it. Not until I was within twenty yards did it fly away, very different from the bird I had seen earlier in the day which seemed excessively shy. The light was too far gone to use my glasses and I could only see, with the naked eye, a dim form against the dark ling clumps and withered grass.

This 'evening calling' seemed a regular feature. Just before sunset they began to cry and continued it well after dark, flying about in little groups on the face of the dark toned plain.

The stone curlew is losing ground and before perhaps another generation has passed, it will have gone the way of the great bustard.

June 22.

Whilst out on Home Guard patrol one sees the world waking up and the birds stirring.

At this time of the year it is scarcely dark. Hardly has the sun gone down, leaving a glow in the western sky, when another paler glow appears in the east. And although this dawn glow takes much longer to increase, the sky is never wholly dark.

It is wonderful to hear the birds begin to tune up, the first always seems to be the lark. Its thin pure notes seem so attuned to the clear freshness of the dawn. At first one begins to sing and then another until the sound of the dropping notes falls like a fine silvery rain. Very soon the blackbirds begin to warble and then the thrushes. In the dawn light the buttercup heads look withered and white, pursed up close against the chill, but in a few hours time when the sun is up they will be full of colour and wide open. These are strange days, or rather nights. The village churches are silenced; they have not been mute since Cromwell's days but they still strike the hour. The sound however has a sinister quality; with the first stroke the senses spring to attention. Yet it is hard to think these gentle summer fields should be under threat of invasion by men so utterly foreign and removed from all the little sacred things we hold so dear.

The light grows slowly, the fields and woods are un-muffled and bird song is redoubled. In the thick chestnuts a few yards from me a blackbird warbles loudly, almost deafeningly so, pure round notes which fill the ear to over-flowing and which seem to dominate the senses and ring inside the head.

The other night I was on the hill opposite. The stars were out and there was a moon, and suddenly from the distant town there came a hideous moaning sound,—the sirens. We could not have devised a more devilish wail than the 'alert'.

I had heard them before many times, in practice tests, but this was the first which told of the dark invader. When it stopped there was nothing but the night wind in the trees and the faint movement of sheep scattered over the bare hill above me. Then came the high drone of an aero-plane. There was something dreadfully sinister in the sound, so high and far away, a pulse beating up among the stars, that spelt of death.

Like silver pales the searchlights sprang out, all together sweeping and searching. Overhead came the plane, heading for the town, and the sound of its engine throbbed to silence. Frantically the searchlights swung, met and passed, now and then lighting up a whitish cloud.

The sheep grazed on, some were lying down, and below in the dark valley a vixen called.

Then from behind the woods arose seven fountains of crimson flame throwing the trees into inky silhouette. For a moment or two there was no sound of any explosion, but I knew that from across the fields the sound was travelling outwards, radiating from those hideous gashes which had now subsided, to leave a faint glare on the low lying clouds. In that silence of waiting I heard the first larks singing high above the wheat fields and then the explosions reached and engulfed me, calamitous sounds that made the ground shudder. The sheep started from their grazing and ran all ways down the hill; the lark's song, which a moment ago had been trembling so high in the freshness of the infant morning, was shocked to silence.

The German plane, after dropping its bombs, came tearing back overhead, reminding me of a nasty little boy who had just thrown a brick through the window of a house and is running away, half gleeful, half afraid of the results of his action.

I saw the 'result' the next day and it was futile and stupid. The bombs had fallen near a railway, digging ugly pocks in a small green meadow. Branches from trees growing in a nearby lane had been ripped from the main trunk as if by the hand of an insane giant. One flying piece of shrapnel had whistled through a heavy iron roller, another, more impish still, had drilled a fowl house narrowly missing a row of sleepy and matronly hens.

And now, July 18, 1940, we wait for the invasion, a fearful joy within our hearts. I think we long to have it over and give the bully some of his own medicine.

With thoughts so busy with war it seems inevitable I should write of it; perhaps in a future time these scrappy notes will be of interest, and one day there will be blessed peace again. Many of us living now may not be here to enjoy it, the folly of it all sickens one.

The truth is we have become far too soft and flabby and with a lazy attitude of mind. I do not think that there is any

Oak in Salcey Forest

C.B.B.

doubt that the motor car has deprived us of healthy exercise and the wireless of true appreciation of music.

Physically, by all accounts, our opponents are a fitter nation, and this is an evil which must be remedied in ourselves after this war is over, if not possible before.

To see our rustics armed with rook rifles and shot guns uncomfortably recalls descriptions of Sedgemoor.

The other night I visited a patrol at 'Number 4 Post' which is on a hill overlooking the Avon valley.

Some very large black poplars grow on the crest of the hill and even on the stillest night one can hear a faint whisper or hiss among the leaves. One of the patrol remarked on the sound, and as we listened it was not difficult to imagine that the sea was below us in the mist. These trees, or rather the sound of them, reminded one of the men of his boyhood days. He had been born in a cottage in the Vale of Evesham and a clump of black poplars grew at the end of the garden.

His father had been a gamekeeper on a big estate close to the village and was a crack shot. It was the latter's duty every autumn to shoot one or two of the best stags for the 'house'. His method was to climb a tree and have the deer driven beneath him.

One day he picked out a fat beast as it ran below and fired. The bullet ricochetted off the horn of the deer and killed a groom who was riding in the park over three hundred yards distant.

In the grounds of this big house there was a lake stocked with very large trout, some six pounds or more in weight. The keepers' boys were allowed to bathe in this pool but not, of course, to fish it.

They soon thought of an original scheme however. Round their ankles they tied long gut casts with a fly attached and then swam across the lake. In this way they caught numbers of good fish, some of great size. One trout my friend caught by this means weighed seven pounds and it nearly played him instead of the other way round.

This new method of poaching was certainly an original idea and deserved success.

I have just been re-reading *Birds and Man*, by Hudson. His little anecdotes, such as the story of the blackbird which was unable to fend for itself and was successfully reared and liberated, is particularly charming.

Now and again I have noticed fledglings of this order, helpless little mites which have either been deserted by their parents or are mentally defectives. For I am sure from my observation of birds, that some are born mentally deficient. These fledglings seem quite unable to fend for themselves. By the laws of nature they have no right to survive and only chance contact with a kindly human foster parent can save their lives.

I have met with several such instances—one a young sparrow which I discovered in my garden, quite unafraid, endeavouring to find some morsels in the weed heads on the lawn. It made no attempt to fly away when I approached and allowed me to pick it up. For some days I fed it on soaked rape seed, small bits of brown bread and hemp seed, and when it was strong enough to fly well and fend for itself I let it go.

In some cases the parent birds will, for no apparent reason, forsake their young and show a marked favouritism for another member of the brood, allowing the unfortunate to starve.

I have had some very dear friends among birds and one or two especially stand out in my mind. One was a linnet which was brought to me as a fledgling. Its feathers had scarcely grown when I took charge and for weeks I laboured to keep it alive. This necessitated early rising, the first feed of the day taking place at six o'clock in the morning. Even that time was far too late, for wild birds begin to feed their young as soon as it gets light in summer. From then onwards throughout the day it was fed at hourly intervals until about seven o'clock at night.

The business of feeding a young wild bird is really hard work for a fortnight, until the youngster can crack hard unsoaked seed for itself. For at least a week the food has to be placed in the mouth, after this they begin to pick up for themselves and the tiresome task is not quite so tedious, though the feeds have to be regular and the early feed is still most necessary. I fed the linnet on brown bread soaked in scalded milk (white bread will soon kill any bird of the finch family) crushed rape seed and boiled hemp.

The hemp was boiled in a rag until the seed, which is rather like a tiny white bulb, split out of the round shell. Small particles of hard boiled egg—the yolk, not the white —is also good, but too much causes constipation. Young birds are like trees or plants which have been dug up and removed to a new place. Some will die however much you work, others, after a few days (whilst their stomachs are adjusting themselves to the unaccustomed food) will thrive. My little linnet managed to survive and one day she cracked her first seed and I knew she would be safe.

Very soon she became so tame that when I opened the cage door she immediately flew out and perched on my shoulder and very soon she developed a character. One or two games she loved to play. Whilst I was writing she would sidle across the table and, waiting her chance, seize hold of the nib of the pen. If this failed she would take hold of the corner of the paper and carry it to the edge of the table and drop it over, standing on the very edge with side-cocked head watching its wavering flight to the floor below. This was quite a feat for so diminutive a bird. Another game was to climb up the collar of my coat and nibble the short hairs in the nape of my neck. Perching on the rim of the collar she would seize a hair between her bill and tug for all she was worth, going back on her heels and putting all her strength in the effort. Sometimes too she would sit directly under my ear and hop up my face; her little feet were always very warm.

Then she would preen my eyebrows, putting each hair in place. The curious thing about this trick was that she never attempted to pull out an eyebrow hair. Like all wild birds she loved her bath which she took in a saucer set on the floor. She soon got to know my step and had a special call note as soon as she heard me enter the house. She could distinguish between my step and another's, even from a distance, and she would fly to no one else. If I walked gently about the room she rode on my shoulder and seemed to enjoy it, though if I quickened my pace or made any swift motion, she flew off. Birds hate any sudden movement and will never become attached to anyone who does not walk or move with a smooth and calculated tread.

She lived for eight years and then one day, when I opened the door of the cage, I saw she was sick. Her feathers were puffed and crest raised. A bird will only raise its head feathers when it is angry, pleased, or ill. The tiny eyes, usually so full and bright and smiling, were like little agates and half their usual size. She flopped out of the cage and rolled into my hand and I felt the little body was chill. There she died and my heart ached with heavy sorrow, a sorrow which remained for weeks.

Perhaps the most lovable pet was a hen bullfinch called Biddy. The nest from which she came was built in some dense thorn bushes at the side of a road and these bushes were being cut down. I knew of the nest and managed to save Biddy before the bushes were felled and incidentally many other little families perished.

Bullfinches are very interesting birds and I think my favourite finch. I have made a special study of them and feel I know the species better than any other British bird. It may seem hard to believe, but I seem to know by instinct

Brooding Bullfinch

where I may find their nests, and it has often happened that whilst motoring or walking along a road bordered by black-thorn I have seen a bush which I felt contained a nest, and on making a search I have found it.

The bullfinch is a secretive bird, loving the dense under-growth of woods and old unkempt hedges and, on the whole, keeps clear of man save in the fruit season when they do quite a lot of damage to the buds.

To return to Biddy—I fetched her at night—this is the best time to take a fledgling—and put her in a warm little basket, and covered her with a scrap of flannel. Most young birds die of cold when taken from the nest, for even when fully fledged, the mother broods them during the dark hours.

I gave her buckwheat crushed and soaked, brown bread and scalded milk, and a little rape seed, and now and again some lettuce chopped up very small and mixed with the food. She seemed to thrive from the first day and was very soon cracking hard seed.

Young bullfinches do not get the black cap until their first moult and it is difficult to tell the sexes apart, though the smaller fledglings are usually the males. Biddy soon developed into a very lovable little person with many of the tricks of the linnet and some more of her own. I was the only person to whom she would fly and she had her own peculiar pipe whenever she heard my step. Like the linnet she loved her bath and she had it every time I let her out into the room. Her greatest treat was to curl up amongst my hair, when my head was resting on the back of the chair, and in this cosy nest would go fast asleep.

The carpet was a great treasure store. Most of her time she would spend gathering enormous moustaches of wool and hairs from the pile, and after accumulating a big bundle would fly to me and bend back her head until her little black Roman nose pointed skywards, uttering a sweet little trilling twitter. This was the action I have seen many times in bullfinches in their wild state when the hen invites the male. She would also do this when I had been out all day and was overjoyed to see me. To have won the love of this tiny wild creature was a wonderful thing to me. To nobody else would she show such affection; I was to her another bird, a giant bullfinch, her mate.

At the height of her ecstasy she would almost close her eyes and her wings would tremble violently all the while.

Then she would shake herself and put her feathers straight and come to my shoulder, where she would sit for as long as I allowed her. One habit she had was to sit on the floor for long periods at a time without moving and this led to a dreadful accident.

One day my father entered the room and never saw her. There was a sickening little scrunch and Biddy lay with a broken leg. I made a little splint by splitting a quill and binding it tightly to the broken limb with thread, and for weeks she hobbled about with this contraption. Then, when the leg was healed, I cut away the splint and found she was as well as ever. But alas! a year or two later, the same thing happened again and this time it was her little body which was crushed and her bright spirit fled for ever.

One more pet must have a place in this little company, Perce, a rook. I found her (despite the name it was really a hen bird) one bright spring afternoon, crouching among the celandines and wood sorrel at the foot of a rookery elm. Some gust of wind or other mischance had precipitated her to the ground below. How long she had lain there I know not but her great red trumpet of a mouth rose from among the spring plants like some exotic orchid. I took her home and placed her in a rush basket liberally lined with hay. Rooks are easily reared, and will eat almost anything, and the rearing of any of the crow family is not so onerous a business as the rearing of a small bird.

Perce throve exceedingly and soon refused to stay in her basket. She would hop about the garden and yards uttering a long drawn caw, as full of mischief as a monkey. When I arrived home in the evening by car the first thing I would see was the black mawkish object hopping like a huge black toad towards me down the drive and, stopping the car, I would take her in and let her sit beside me.

She mostly spent the day under some lilac bushes, or feeding on a little lawn nearby where she dug for worms with her heavy pointed bill. Her chief delight was to steal up behind some unsuspecting person and sharply tweak their ankles. Or she would seize hold of a shoe lace and endeavour to undo the knot. She regarded other people with a reserved suspicion; to me she showed a touching devotion which was almost doglike. It is strange to think a bird can show love which we seem to think is.a purely human thing. For me she smiled, looking up into my eyes, never at my legs, hands, or body, eye to eye was her love transmitted. When a bird smiles the lower membrane is slightly raised and the crest also. For me she had a sweet and tuneful note which was quite a different sound from the usual harsh 'caw'. Soon she could fly, but she never went far away from the house or garden. Some days she would not be there to meet me in the drive and I would go in search of her, calling her name, Perce! Perce! And very soon from the loft or stable I would hear her answer with a loud prolonged 'caw' which was her greeting. On seeing me, her delight was touching. With great bounding hops she would rush to meet me and, when she had reached my feet, would look up into my face, bowing until her bill touched the ground, fanning her tail and spreading her wings. This performance was a regular thing and I was the only one to receive her homage. Then came the day when no black gnome awaited me in the drive and no voice answered when I called. I went round all her favourite haunts; by the lilac bushes; in the garage where she used to roost on a heap of old tyres; up in the laundry and the workshop above it, to which she climbed by way of the stairs. Stair climbing was her great delight. If she could get into the house she would climb to the top landing and as it was a three storied house she had about forty steps to ascend. And then the search was made over wider fields, in the garden, the paddock, everywhere. But Perce had disappeared.

Four days she was missing and then one evening something made me call to her again and from a dark corner of the saddle-room I heard a weak 'caw'. There was Perce, thin, so weak she could scarcely stand, and with one wing dragging and broken.

What dark incident had overtaken her we never knew. Perhaps some dog or cat had attacked her, or perhaps she had become entangled in a trap. We nursed her carefully back to health, putting her in the warm basket which had been her nest as a fledgling. But never again did she leave the close proximity of the house or even venture down the drive to greet me.

Instead, she spent most of her day in the scullery or the kitchen, plaguing the life out of the cook and frightening the maids. The wing never healed and she could not fly, but her love for me was as strong as ever.

During her second year we had an influx of rats and mice. We put down rat poison in the outhouses and the rats came out to die. Perce, always a snapper up of unconsidered trifles, partook liberally of a mouse which had come out of its hole to die and the next day Perce was sick. She consumed large quantities of water and refused all solid food. Slowly she pined away, getting thinner and thinner each day, and then one morning I went out to see her and found she had died in the night.

The story began among the celandines that soft spring morning had been written and I had lost a very loving soul.

Cock birds are never so affectionate as hens, why this should be is hard to understand. All wild birds, if reared as a brood and not singly, are never so tame and do not develop the same individual characters.

Though the interior of a young bird's mouth is usually yellow, that of the young bullfinch is in a class apart. It is of a deep carmine colour with curious yellow markings on the roof. Some naturalists say that this is to scare away any marauding creature which appears over the rim of the nest, in the same way that the face of the puss moth caterpillar is supposed to frighten birds which attempt to eat it. Even in their wild state they are most affectionate birds and will mate for life; they also keep their young with them, long after they have left the nest, and like the longtailed tits, the family will sometimes keep together all through the winter months, roosting in the same place at night for warmth, and feeding in the same locality.

There can be no prettier sight than a family party of bullfinches in late autumn when the red berries glow against the hedge, and the twigs have taken on that soft purple bloom which seems almost like a mist. The soft pink of the male bird's breast harmonizes beautifully with its surroundings. It is a picture I have seen again and again.

As I sit now in this sunny little room in late July and look out of the window at the strong breeze turning the leaves so that they show their pale undersides against the strong blue sky, my thoughts go back in memory to many a winter and autumn walk when I have seen the bullfinch families enjoying the hedgerow berries. They like deserted roadways and spinneys. There are many such deserted lanes about here in Warwickshire, old coaching tracks now green with sward which I describe in a later chapter.

Rambling along the lanes, which are usually bounded on either side by high unkept hedges, one sees many varieties of birds; redstarts, finches, and linnets (though not the goldfinch, who prefers the outskirts of the village where there is more life and apple blossom), whitethroats and willow warblers, chiff-chaffs and tree pipits. The latter bird, like the bullfinch, is very fond of deserted and derelict roads. The male bird has his own particular tree from which he sings, 'parachuting' down with spread tail. It is fairly common in Warwickshire. I was once told by a very keen ornithologist who collected wild birds' eggs that one can always find a tree pipit's nest if the 'singing tree' of the cock bird is discovered. The nest is apparently always within a certain distance and within a given radius. It is cleverly hidden and rarely found except when the hen flutters out at one's feet.

Away from these deserted roads, along the railway banks, the commonest bird is the whinchat. Close by my house, on the railway, there are to my knowledge three nesting pairs within a mile. They are anxious, nervous birds, and the cock keeps constant watch during the incubating period, either from a nearby tree top or from the telegraph wire.

The whinchat's nest is even harder to find than that of the tree pipit and the hen sits closely.

Near this certain stretch of railway I have in mind there is a marsh where I often find a snipe or two in the winter. At first sight it should be a first-class place for duck, but strange to say, though there is a big reservoir not far away and duck constantly pass over, they never alight there, even in the hardest weather.

This reservoir, which is comparatively new, is a very fine place for birds. At one point the water is shallow; the valley was damned at one end and the water allowed to flood back, converting what was once waste meadow into a lake. It is shallow enough for duck to feed in, by upending they can easily touch the bottom and consequently, in the winter especially, thousands of wildfowl frequent it, ducks of all kinds, including shovellers and vast companies of widgeon and now and again some of the rarer grebes.

A year ago, one June afternoon, I saw what appeared to be a very large black swallow catching flies just above the surface of the water. It was a black tern, a very rare visitor to these inland waters.

The Avon which feeds the reservoir holds some quite large perch and I spend odd hours fishing for them. Perch, though many people are not aware of the fact, are perfectly delicious eating, almost equal to a trout if caught in clear-bottomed water such as this reservoir. They require room and depth to attain any size. I have a theory that most of the roach and perch in the reservoir come up the Avon to breed. The river is only a small stream here and for quite a way up the river valley the shallows are swarming with perch and roach fry.

My old friend, the crossing keeper, sometimes comes fishing with me. His job is, perhaps, the most wretched and thankless task, opening the gates by hand whenever any vehicle uses the narrow road; up at all hours and never sure of a good night's rest. Yet he always has a smile and it does one good to see his cheery red face. Whatever the weather, or however black the news, Mr. Kant always has a smile and a joke. He is one of the most generous of men; sometimes when I am passing he comes to the car window and says, 'Will you take a boiling of my taters, they're beauties', and out comes his wife with a basket full. Sometimes when I come home from shooting he will ask me in for a cup of tea and in these days of rationing it is no small thing to dispense hospitality. For fifteen years he has opened the crossing gates. On Sunday evenings he takes his rod and tin of worms and goes after the perch. It has become quite a regular thing now for my wife and I to join him and he looks forward to it all the week, and so do we.

About three years ago Kant had a stroke of luck. One morning a letter arrived to say he had won a considerable sum of money in a football pool (I think it was about £200), and the first thing he did was to give a large donation to the local hospital.

Here was a poor man (if you count wealth as riches) and his first thought was to give to charity. Probably he had never had so much money before, and never would again, but he gave a quarter of it away.

'What did you do with the rest, Kant'? I asked.

'Why sir I put it away in the bank and it pays for our holidays every summer.'

His 'holidays' consist of one week in the year.

Sometimes when I miss a perch, he ejaculates, 'well, swelp my taters'.

I know that Mr. Kant has solved a very big problem, that of human happiness. By some of our standards he is in fact a very wealthy man. By contentment with a simple life and a steadfast cheerfulness in all things, he has, I am sure, found the secret of successful living and he possesses that all too rare a thing, a kindly heart.

Considerate folk do not use the road after dark, for it means the old man has to get out of bed and come down to open the gates and set the signal; this is a beastly business on a winter's night. Others, not so considerate, will get him up, and sometimes tipsy roysterers hoot loudly in the small hours and he has to let them through, half frozen fingers fumbling with the heavy padlock. But Mr. Kant never ceases to smile and has no grudge against any man.

During this last winter he was snowed in for over a week and the line blocked by deep drifts. Even Kant, who is an old man, could not remember a winter like it. Luckily he had stores of food in the house, otherwise they would have been in a difficult, even serious, position.

I sometimes think that if a German bomber was to lay an

egg on the crossing and demolish Kant's house about his ears, all he would say would be 'swelp my taters', and keep on smiling.

Young Bullfinch

CHAPTER IV

A Forest Ride

Chapter IV

Just before the present war I made a journey on a German cargo boat to Lithuania and Latvia. It would be out of place in a book such as this to describe the journey and of the various adventures (some quite exciting) which befell me, but I was able to accumulate some interesting natural history notes.

Whilst at Memel I had one particularly memorable ramble in the dense pine forests inland.

The country is sandy and fairly flat, heavily timbered by dwarf scrub pine. One very hot day I walked with a friend across this forest country. Everywhere I noticed the sweet, somewhat sickly, scent of the pine trees and this perfume was noticeable far out to sea. One species of crow was excessively common, a bird not unlike our hoodie crow, though larger and with a biscuit coloured mantle. Not only did we see them in the forests but about the quays and town of Riga.

On this particular day we tramped many miles and a very hot business it was. Underfoot the sand was loose and uncomfortable for walking, even under the pines it was heated by the sun. Near the sea we came to rolling dunes covered with a species of close growing lichen and here I saw a small golden fritillary fly past. It settled on a sunlit patch of sand and stealing up I saw it with wings outspread. It was a Queen of Spain fritillary, an insect I had never seen before. This richly marked butterfly is extremely beautiful, indeed I am not sure it is not more attractive than any of the species we find in Britain. Close to the dunes I found a great number of them and graylings were also common.

I have only once met an entomologist who has seen this fritillary in England and his story was a curious one. It happened that one day, whilst butterfly hunting near Sywell wood in Northamptonshire (once a well-known locality and since cut down), he was standing on the edge of the woods waiting for anything that chanced along. The rays of the sun beat down with such power that he had put over his head a white handkerchief. Suddenly a small golden butterfly appeared and flew close by him. Imagine his excitement when he saw that it was a Queen of Spain! His net was ready but the butterfly eluded it and circled round his head. For a moment he stood, not knowing what to do, and then an unbelievable thing happened. The insect settled on the white handkerchief on his head and he stood, not knowing what to do. Naturally he could not hope to catch it whilst it remained there and a second later it flew off and he missed it. Away it went, dancing over the corn field and that was the last that he saw of it!

After wandering about for some time we went back to the forest and in a clearing, shadow dappled, a large black butterfly swept past. In an instant I saw it was a Camberwell Beauty. It settled on the trunk of a pine tree in a patch of sunlight, opening and shutting its glorious wings, the most lovely butterfly I have ever seen.

This was the only one I saw during my stay at Memel, but as it was late in the season it is probable that, like the Queen of Spain, it is common in that part of the world. The specimen I saw was in perfect condition and must have been newly hatched.

I saw many species of birds unknown to me in the woods, mostly small warblers with distinctive wing barrings. And I also noticed crossbills. The pine trees were nowhere of great height and nearly all were clothed and draped with long grey lichens. Later I learnt that wolves, bears, and wild boars are by no means uncommon during the winter months. I only wished that I had longer to explore the country, but we were only in Memel for a few days and I never had the opportunity.

Somehow butterflies seen abroad do not give me the same thrill which I get from those at home and the same applies to birds. Our butterfly family is woefully small when compared to other countries and Scotland and Ireland are very poorly off for both birds and butterflies. I never get the same joy from those gorgeous Indian insects one sees in collections. Surpassingly lovely as they are, both in form and colour, I would rather see a Large Blue or a Swallow Tail here at home. The tropical birds and butterflies are too exotic, almost vulgar; it is like comparing an orchid to a speedwell.

I have written a good deal in the past about woods and woodlands, and never tire of talking about them because they attract me so. To be alone among the trees, whether in winter or summer, is a constant delight. I say alone, because that is the only way you can enjoy a wood; a companion, even one's closest friend, takes away something of that sense of adventure which I always feel is caught in the shadows of the branches.

Fortunately in this and the adjoining county, there are very big woods and the country is very heavily timbered.

Trees, like streams, are always interesting, and constantly change from day to day according to the season.

I have just come in from a ramble in Wappenbury forest. All woods have characters of their own; this is composed mostly of birches but there are a few oaks, small trees as yet, though I suspect that at one time it was composed entirely of the latter trees. Here and there are ridings, or rather paths, because in no place could a waggon pass through. These paths are sometimes almost shut in by the surrounding undergrowth, though occasionally spaces open out, shoulder high with green bracken fronds.

The birch trees are mostly the black variety which seem to grow more in bushes than trees, and are not nearly so graceful. But nevertheless it is a very lovely wood.

When I arrived there this afternoon it was raining quite heavily, and it seemed more like April than July. I stood under the birches, as I had no overcoat or mac, but became nearly as wet as if I had been out in the open. The birch gives little or no shelter, as the leaves are so neat and round.

After a while the dark clouds blew over and the sun blazed forth and in an incredibly short time it had dried the leaves and grass. As soon as the warm glow smote the bramble bush in front of me I saw a brown and white object crawling up the stem. It was a butterfly, a draggled White Admiral. After two or three days of flight these butterflies get very knocked about, with small triangles nicked out of their wings, possibly by dragonflies and birds, for the White Admiral is very distinctive. Then a lovely flash of gold came past, a male Silver Washed fritillary, one of the most lovely of all our native butterflies.

I shall never forget a most unique sight I saw last year, one hot afternoon in July, in another much nobler forest in the adjoining county.

The scene was laid in a wide and majestic riding in which grew tall thistles. On either side were the ancient oaks, great rough barked trees of ample girth with wild bramble bushes round their feet.

On one blackberry bush, in full sunlight, there was a moving curtain of tawny gold, the colour of ripe corn. There must have been fully thirty or forty Silver Washed fritillaries on that bush, some of the dark bronze-green variety which is known as Valezina. Here and there was a White Admiral, a draggled specimen, for it was getting late in the season for them. I just stood and feasted my eyes on the scene and revelled in it. Some of the butterflies must have been newly out for they were without blemish, with a beautiful gloss or bloom on the powdery hairs close to the body. The rich tawny gold of the wings, accentuated by the dark blackish markings seemed to leap out of the green and white background, burning as if they were gold flames. But to return to my rambles in Wappenbury.

Now that the sun was shining, butterflies appeared on all sides; Commas, Tortoiseshells, and Fritillaries, and high up the foliage of the birches and oaks, White Admirals floated round with an airy gliding flight.

There is no other butterfly which has such surpassing beauty of flight, they are almost bird-like. Everywhere too Meadow Browns and Ringlets were on the wing; the latter seem to be about even when rain is falling.

I took a woodland path and was soon lost in the very heart of this lovely wilderness.

Under the overhanging branches the ground was soaking wet and the long grass drenched the legs of my trousers. I stopped in a little clearing and saw, close beside me on a birch twig, a green caterpillar which harmonized beautifully with the tender green of the birch trees. It was quite a large creature with an imposing horn which identified it as belonging to the hawk moth tribe, and on closer inspection so it proved to be, a broad bordered bee hawk caterpillar.

After becoming soaked from the waist downwards I retraced my steps and in a very short time completely lost my sense of direction and did not know how I could get out of the wood. It is surprisingly easy to lose one's way in these densely timbered woodlands, and though I have a pretty good bump of locality it was some time before I got back to the original blackberry bush where I had seen the White Admiral.

As soon as I got there I saw another, almost a perfect specimen, sunning itself on a blackberry flower, a male Silver Washed close beside it.

I came up with two Rugby boys armed with nets and we fell to talking. They were very keen and both had good collections. 'What is your rarest butterfly'? I asked one of them.

'Oh, a Camberwell Beauty.'

And I heard the whole story how, in an old Oxford garden, he had caught a perfect specimen of this rare insect. The gardener had told him of a queer looking butterfly with yellow borders to its dark wings, which he had seen flopping round a pear tree.

He had raced indoors for his net, and sure enough, on his return there was a Camberwell Beauty feeding on some rotten pears which had fallen to the grass.

I had only once seen this butterfly in its wild state and that was in Lithuania, as described earlier in these notes.

There is something very like the Red Admiral in the habits of the Camberwell Beauty, both love rotten fruit and old world gardens, and they each have the same flopping flight.

White Admiral on Honeysuckle Spray

Talking of butterflies reminds me that I saw an amazing sight the other morning near Rugby. A field of oats nearly ripe was bending in the breeze and dancing above it, as far as the eye could see, were thousands upon thousands of white cabbage butterflies. And a little farther along the road I saw thousands more, all moving across the field in an easterly direction. No doubt they were on migration, for butterflies as well as birds migrate and they cover vast distances. The sight of the grey green crop with the millions of white scraps dancing above it made a lovely picture.

How strange it is that butterflies should have the migrating instinct, as it seems unbelievable that they can cross wide seas. The same fate that overtakes migrating birds must be the same for butterflies; adverse winds and wild weather means the death of millions.

I have told in another book how, when I was on a trawler fishing near the Dogger Bank, a butterfly in the last stages of exhaustion tried to reach the ship. We were moving before a fair breeze and for a long while it could make no progress. Slowly however it forged ahead, though flying lower and lower all the time, until, when almost at the boat, it fell on to the sea and rested there with closed wings. Those two little brown wings, closed like praying hands, was the last I saw of the butterfly as a larger wave than the others hid it from view.

The Comma, which species I mentioned earlier in the chapter, is excessively common this year (1940) in Wappenbury woods; numbers of my friends have taken them and I saw a good many this afternoon.

One wood pile overgrown with blackberry blossom was alive with Tortoiseshells and Commas. As I am on the subject of butterflies I am reminded of a parson friend of mine whose great hobby is butterfly collecting. Perhaps he is the sort of man whom Hudson would dislike, for this great naturalist was against collecting in any form, and I am inclined to agree with him. But my friend certainly has a very fine array which he has caught himself. He told me that years ago his great delight was to get the pupae of Swallow Tails and Large Blue butterflies, and hatch them out. Then he liberated them in the room and would watch them fly about.

Last year I made a special journey to Monk's Wood, in Huntingdonshire, a most famous locality for all kinds of butterflies and moths. Much has been cut down, but it is still a very good place for many of the rarer kinds. I was disappointed in the place, indeed it is one of the few woods which repelled me, why I cannot say. It appeared to me to be a swampy sort of wood with little undergrowth and with a great many ash trees, a tree I do not particularly admire.

Down one of the ridings I met a lovely character, an entomologist of the old school, complete with an 'emperor' net some fifteen feet high. What amused me was his pretended ignorance of butterflies, and his sly thirst for information suggested that he was a professional collector.

Monk's Wood is mentioned in all the butterfly books of note, but like many another locality, its best days are over. Why certain species of butterflies should suddenly become rare or disappear altogether is quite inexplicable.

Some species like the White Admiral have increased enormously in recent years, though a short while back it was confined to a few localities in the south. Another case is that of the Comma. Not very long ago the capture of this butterfly was quite an event, now it is comparatively plentiful. The Black Veined White used to be commonly taken during the early part of the last century, now it is practically extinct. Why should this be? The reason is not always connected with the food plant. Perhaps from time to time disease sets in, wiping out a certain species.

The case of the Large Copper is an interesting one. I have just been lent a paper on this butterfly and it makes most fascinating reading. The caterpillar is apparently able to live under the water for a considerable length of time, which may be as long as ten days or a fortnight. As the district where the Large Copper is found (it has been re-introduced into the fen country) is subjected to floods, this must be a case of adaption on the part of the larvae.

The disappearance of the Large Blue from such localities as Barnwell Wold (a locality I know well) can be explained by the fact that sheep are no longer pastured there and consequently its food plant (wild thyme) has disappeared. What was once close clipped grassland is now a tangled wilderness of rush and thorn scrub. But it is still a fine locality for the entomologist and I have seen there three different species of fritillaries on the wing at once; Silver Washed, High Brown, and Dark Green.

In reading books on entomology one is struck by the fact that some species, especially of the moths, have only been discovered during the last half-century. This makes one wonder if there are not other species waiting to be revealed, some dingy little moth which has its home in some remote wood or faraway mountainside.

There must be numbers of rare butterflies seen every year by people who know nothing about entomology. A Black Veined White for instance would never be noticed, or a Large Blue might be any other 'blue' to the ignorant eye.

The chances of a rare butterfly being seen, especially of the smaller and less insignificant species, are very remote. I was told, only the other day, of a locality where the Large Blue is found in comparative abundance, but wild horses will not drag from me the name of the place. It was dis-covered quite by accident by my friend who was spending a holiday there. I can well imagine the thrill he experienced when, walking along a rough hillside in a certain valley, he saw his first 'wild' Large Blue fly past. Of course he found it hard to believe his eyes, but before the afternoon was over he had seen any number of this very lovely little butterfly.

One day I hope to travel to that same spot and see them for myself; the knowledge that the place is only known to my friend and myself will add to the enjoyment.

Purple Emperor

For were I to publish the locality, or even the county, the entomologist would ferret it out, and my precious scraps of blue would be no more. So it is no good any reader, who covets this knowledge of mine, writing to me for I will never part with the secret.

Some species keep very much to a certain locality, sometimes only a few fields, and they never stray beyond. An instance of this is the Marbled White. I know of one locality in my neighbourhood where this very lovely insect is found, and I never see it beyond a certain hedge and one particular lane.

Though Northamptonshire is given in all the butterfly books as a county where the Purple Emperor may still be found I have only seen it on one or two occasions.

Talking of the Purple Emperor reminds me again of Monk's Wood. This used to be a great place for this insect, and three years ago a friend of mine, whilst motoring through the wood (a road runs right through it) saw a fine specimen sitting on some horse manure in the middle of the road. He had no net with him and a swoop of the hat failed to procure it. He had the chagrin of seeing the regal insect mounting up to the top of the nearest oak tree.

August 3.

A forest day. A lovely cloudless summer morning, one of the loveliest that ever came out of God's heaven, and to think that men are killing each other, it is monstrous and quite unbelievable.

I reached the forest at ten-thirty a.m. There was a faint dew on the grass, not enough to wet the shoes as there will be later in the month, but enough to bring out all the fragrant scents of woodland ride and underbrush.

As always, my quest was for Aputra Iris (the Purple Emperor). This insect has become for me a lovely and elusive prize which I sometimes think I shall never find here. Once I thought I saw it in this forest, some years ago, a fleeting black shape rising above the top of a high oak, but there is always the haunting thought that it might have been a Large Tortoiseshell or an outsize in Red Admirals.

In the old butterfly books it is amusing to read of how the ancient entomologists describe the Purple Emperor— 'allied sovereigns', 'their imperial majesties', and the like.

What true hunter of 'flies' can read unmoved of that hot summer day, so long ago in time, when the Rev. William Bree chased and caught a Purple Emperor, in his hat, down a riding at Ashton Wold! I have seen that very riding where the perspiring Rev. gentleman pursued his prize, the oaks are still there and maybe a Purple Emperor too when the July sun blazes down. I suppose generations of Oundle boys have visited the spot; very few will have seen an Emperor.

Most of these ancient records mention Northamptonshire. A paper just lent me tells of an Emperor being seen and captured at Yardley Chase near Northampton, and of another, captured by a gamekeeper, in Geddington Chase near Kettering.

I thought of these ancient records as I walked quietly down the ride, scanning the tops of the oaks on either side. With my powerful glasses I could project my eye, as it were, almost among the topmost leaves, where I could see the bees and flies settling on the upper walls of foliage.

But no flapping shape rewarded my search and after a while I turned to the sallows growing along the edge of the riding. The sallow, which is the food plant of the Emperor, grows abundantly in this locality and it seems strange that Iris should be so rare. In all my wanderings in this forest I have never met a fellow butterfly hunter and even if the Emperors were there I doubt whether anyone save myself would see them.

Now and then a flash of corn gold passed along the curtain of foliage, bathed now in the hot sunlight. These Silver Washed fritillaries were past their best, most were torn and frayed. If you want a perfect specimen you must come earlier in the year, in June, when they are newly out. I searched the sallow bushes methodically but found no infant larvae. In the latter half of July they would be very small and easily missed.

Probably because of its association with the Emperor the sallow always attracts me. Parting the slender wands I let my eye rove round the interior of the bushes but I could not find a caterpillar of any description. This was strange as numbers of leaves had been eaten, some right down to the main rib. Beyond some curious little brown hammer-headed beetles however I found nothing.

Some of the sallows were young and juicy, fresh clean-limbed rods bearing luscious almond shaped leaves, others were old and moth eaten, yet I searched all I could see on either side of the riding.

At the edge of the path, flowers of all kinds grew in a perfect wall; knapweeds with their crimson heads, each with a sidling peacock butterfly, so it seemed, thistles and above all, regiments of meadow sweet; its crumbly whitish yellow flowers scented the air. Butterflies do not seem to like this fragrant flower, though occasionally I saw a tattered fritillary (Silver Washed) settle upon it.

Wild hemlock was common, handsome sturdy plants which grew well over six feet in places, their flat umbrellas crawling with long red beetles. The beetle family is such a large one that were I to study them I should have no time left for birds or butterflies and the latter interest me far more. I did however find an amazing beetle which, by its beauty, almost took my breath away. It was on a knapweed head.

I was walking along and suddenly my eye was arrested by a scintillating jewel which seemed to reflect the rays of the sun. On looking more closely I saw a small round beetle about the size of a ladybird. It seemed exactly like some precious stone or jewel, crusted with iridescent green and silver. I wished I knew its name.

On some blackberry blossom I saw no less than four Comma butterflies, all perfect specimens newly hatched and without a tear in their curious jig-saw wings. The colour of

G   C.B.B.

the Comma always reminds me of an unripe blackberry, it is a ruddier tinge than the Tortoiseshell and more beautiful.

Flitting round the sapling oaks I could see, through the glasses, numberless hair streaks, probably Purple Hair Streaks. These odd little butterflies seem to spend their time around the upper oak leaves and rarely venture down within reach of the net. When I scanned the higher oaks I could see others. The Purple Hair Streak has the same habits as the Purple Emperor and the same purple glory on the wings.

The woodland path went on and on, turning this way and that, beckoning mysteriously. Here was a clearing bathed in sunlight, the stems of the plants dry and brittle, though where the forest crowded in on either hand the grass and flowers were still wet with the morning dew.

A few Brimstones were out, like the Commas, newly hatched, and without tear or blemish. Were it a rare butterfly the Brimstone would indeed be a prize. Barring the Swallow Tail no other British butterfly has such wonderfully shaped wings.

Now and again I would scan the upper oaks for 'His Imperial Majesty' and once, when I saw a large black butterfly floating about in the sunlight round the top of a very high oak, I thought I had found him. But it was such a fleeting glimpse I could not be sure.

Then the path took a sharp turn to the right and again to the left and quite suddenly I found myself in a large clearing in the very heart of the forest. And there, half-hidden in with sallow bushes and oaks, was a tiny house which might have come out of a fairy story. Its roof was not made of sugar, though it might well have been, and when I peered through the cobwebby windows I could see and hear no witch within. I should not have been surprised if I had heard a thin piping voice inviting me to enter. Who could have lived here in the very middle of this great forest? How came it that men should build a house so far from the world of men?

Weeds grew right up to the windows, half covering them, berry-laden alders choked the front door, the interior was dim and dark, the door locked with a rusty lock. Behind the house were the remains of an old dog kennel, quite a large one, with the iron pales red with rust.

Perhaps this was a keeper's house, relic of the old and stately days when this was a royal hunting forest.

I thought that I could be happy here, living the life of a hermit and a hunter, surrounded by trees. What beauty would be mine, I should be living in the core of it. What glory in autumn when the leaves had turned, what adventure in the summer nights! And I thought of the winter, when the forest was under snow, and the doings of the woodland creatures could be read in their lacing footprints.

I should like to have taken that house and made it habitable, the very ideal of a week-end cottage!

I wandered off into the clearing, into the full blaze and fire of the sunlight. There was no moisture here, not a drop. Knapweeds made a purple carpet and Tortoiseshells and Common Blues were everywhere. On the other side of the clearing was a veritable jungle of sallow which would take a month to search. And above it were ancient oaks, the very oldest trees in the whole forest, but the searching glasses revealed no Emperor dancing round their hoary crowns.

There was a sleepy peace in that hot place, the crickets whizzed and shrilled in the dry grass and over the rim of the surrounding trees small fluffy clouds, like cherubs, floated against a ceiling of deepest blue.

A pigeon arrowed across the sky followed by a hawk. At my feet, caught in the dead grasses, was a spotted and barred owl's feather.

It was with reluctance I said goodbye to my enchanted house and the July forest, and as the shadows lengthened I made my way back along the ridings to the road. On the way I came across a family of Wood Whites, a very local little insect which is however extremely common in this place. Many collectors would travel miles to capture this floppy, dull little creature. They have no beauty of flight, they seem half drunk, like the autumn flies. Yet on close inspection they are quite attractive with slender grey bodies and fairy-like wings.

.   .   .   .

To the South of Northampton there is a wonderful stretch of wild forest country known as Yardley Chase. In years gone by this was one vast forest, haunt of the deer and boar, though little now remains of the original trees.

Here and there however, growing in the middle of the fields, are huge gnarled oaks, hollow in the centre, with only the outer skin remaining. Cowper's Oak is one of these, the tree under which Northamptonshire's only poet of note was wont to compose his lines. When I visited the tree recently on a very hot day, some ten or a dozen sheep were dozing inside it, where they were out of the burning rays of the sun.

Cowper's Oak will stand for many years yet, unless a Nazi bomb uproots it. The original tree must have been impressive, but the passage of years has worn it down until it is now a mere shell, though its upper branches are still green.

Other ancient oaks in the close vicinity, which must be quite as old as Cowper's Oak, perhaps older, are truly dead, with no green leaves or live branches. These trees remind me of those water worn stumps which are cast up upon the shore by storms, and indeed they are comparable, for they have been worn away by the waves of time, by the sun of summer and the winds of winter. Nearly all have hollow interiors as big as barns and the earth inside is pocked and punched by the hooves of cattle and sheep.

In such a country one may expect to find Aputra Iris. All about are great woods, mostly of oak and with a fine underbrush of sallow.

From Yardley Hastings the road deteriorates into a rutted track flanked on either hand by wild and heathy country, pink with loosestrife and silver with thistles, with here and there banks of knapweed and golden rod, in short, a grand place for butterflies. But it is not here you will look for Aputra Iris but in those far woods yonder that show in a hazy line of foliage against the sky.

Soon the track becomes turf grown and is gated. At length it disappears altogether and one walks over the smooth green sward. Leaving my car at the farm house I passed Cowper's Oak and saw before me a stretch of the old forest, bisected with wide ridings. No more suitable place for Iris could be found, for the sallow grew along every riding edge and the oaks were high, their heavy green crowns hazy in the July heat.

Strange to say however I found the wood singularly devoid of life of any sort, even birds seemed absent and only common Meadow Browns and a Comma or two flitted about the bushes. Farther inside the wood I saw a few tattered fritillaries and some Holly Blues but nothing else. After a while my eyes ached through scanning the oak tops with my glasses.

It was an 'up and down' wood, by that I mean the ride dipped into deep hollows with the trees on either hand, and eventually became narrower until the path was almost choked with sallow bushes. The only thing I saw here was a flirtation between a male Silver Washed Fritillary and a female of the same species. This was strange, as the mating season was long past. After a while heat haze covered the sun and all the forest fell asleep, not a bird stirred, even the bobbing Meadow Browns vanished. I returned to the car and had my lunch by a little mound. Close by was a pond, a most fascinating place. It was in the form of a letter L, and in the middle was a green mound on which grew a very old oak tree with its roots clawing down into the water, which appeared quite deep. No doubt it had been sown on the mound by a bird, a pheasant perhaps or a rook.

I thought there must be bushels of acorns in that pond and tons of leaves, enough to fill it right up. You will frequently find trees in the vicinity of ponds, for birds are always about them, coming to drink and bathe on the hot summer days. There was a wasp's nest close to the tree in a sandy bluff, and my glass of beer attracted many of them. Some people say the wasp is always a gentleman and will not sting unless molested. This is not true as I have myself been stung by a wasp without any provocation whatever. They have hasty tempers. As to the old Bumble bees, humming their way along like big striped threshing machines, they will not hurt anyone, though they are irritable, as well they might be, seeing that they work so hard and with so much industry.

I tried to picture the forest in Cowper's time. It was not difficult to do this for wherever one looked one could see solitary oak trees of enormous girth, some of them standing in the centre of the fields with cattle grouped under them.

Giving up any thought of seeing Iris in this part of the forest I set my course for another big wood on the horizon, Ravenstone. No doubt ravens were common about here a century or two ago, hence the name.

It was a very hot walk and a rough road. Much of the original woodland had been cut down and I followed the old cart track, down which they drew the timber in the long wagons; the horses' hooves had poached the ground into deep holes. Grass had grown over and every now and then the foot caught in one of them.

Every variety of flower seemed to be growing on either side of the track. Regiments of willow herb and seas of silver thistle, but few butterflies were seen, only seven magnificent Peacocks on a clump of knapweed. These butterflies seem especially fond of knapweed.

A very wide ride cuts Ravenstone in two; it might be a bit of the New Forest. Here surely I should see Iris! It was so hot I had to throw myself down in the shade of some sallow bushes and rest.

Though I walked the length of the ride however the only thing I saw was a Valenzina variety of the Silver Washed which I was unable to catch.

Brimstones were seen, and from their perfect condition must have been newly hatched. A friend of mine once caught a strange aberration of a Brimstone. Instead of the usual bright lemon yellow, its wings were clouded with a greenish tinge and spotted with a rather lovely rusty red. He had been offered five pounds for this aberration. Apparently Brimstones very rarely throw freaks. This particular butterfly he had caught in his own garden.

Looking through the records one is struck by the fact that so many of the old naturalists were country parsons. The profession of a country clergyman in most cases allows of a great deal of spare time. Old gentlemen like Gilbert White and C. A. Johns are in the front rank of first class naturalists because they had the leisure to observe wild animals and birds. Even today I know a great many country parsons who are observant and good naturalists.

It has been a wonderful harvest this year. Despite the iron winter, or maybe because of it, the fields are full of golden crops, mostly stooked up now (August 17) with wheat, oats,

and barley. Today it has been extremely hot and all afternoon I have noted the pigeons passing over, bound for
Major Howard's crops. As he has asked me to shoot them I
got out my twelve bore and fifty cartridges and walked
across to the farm. During the afternoon the sun was so hot
I could not pluck up enough courage to face a long vigil,
surrounded by prickly stooks, right in the centre of the
field, so I waited until after tea.

As I went down through the farm yard I saw the
swallows hawking round the barns, swinging up and down
in the hot air, their blue shadows crossing and re-crossing
the lichen-stained tiles.

Along the ridge of the roof a row of young swallows were
waiting to be fed and as the parent birds swept by they
turned their little knob-like heads in unison.

Soon I saw the cornfield with its neat rows of stooks, each
with its patch of shade lying across the stubble. A strong
covey of partridges got up as I opened the five barred gate.
Blue clouds of pigeons arose from the field and from a tall
ash growing in the hedge-row many more flew away. This
was the place where I would build my hide. You will shoot
more pigeons from a hide built within range of such a tree
than you will if you go out into the centre of the field. Most
hedge-rows bordering corn fields have a tall tree growing
in them and invariably pigeons will settle there before
dropping down on to the sheaves. It did not take me long to
build a snug hiding place in the middle of the hedge about
thirty yards from the ash tree. I trampled down the stinging
nettles and soon had a comfortable place surrounded by
sheaves of barley.

Barley stooks are most uncomfortable to handle, the long
thin whiskers at the end of the ears break off into little
pieces which will work through the thickest material.

I set up a stuffed decoy on the top of a stook out in the

field and lighting a pipe settled down to wait. Looking out over the quiet scene, with the golden stubble and the little village beyond, crowned by the square tower, it was hard to believe we were at war. There was an unbelievable peace in this very English scene. Near the horizon the sky was pinkish grey with quivering heat and distant trees danced in the mirage.

Two wall butterflies, a male and a female, came bobbing past and settled in a sunlit patch close by. The male advanced towards the female which immediately began to shiver its wings violently. He then jumped repeatedly forward, bumping the female on the nose. This performance went on for five minutes until the male flew away, leaving the female still sitting, shivering its wings.

Soon a pigeon passed me, wheeled, and swept back its wings, diving down towards the ash. Seen from the front, the set wings of a pigeon are held very high on the body and the bird rushes downwards at an incredible speed. This offers a most difficult shot, but I was successful, and it fell out in the field between two stooks. Very soon I had seven pigeons in the hide and the shade from the ash tree had stretched far across the stubble. No more birds came, so I packed up and went home.

.   .   .   .

I stood tonight at the top of the little marsh on my shoot, waiting for duck.

The long hot summer is over, many of the bushes were beginning to turn colour and a few pale slivers had dropped on to the boggy margin of the brook, others had fallen in and been carried away downstream. The dry weather has shrunk the water courses and most of the field ponds are dry. As I waited there I thought of all the sunshiny hours we have had during the last twelve weeks and how the glorious rays must have poured on to this quiet little backwater in the meadows. There was a strand of sheep's wool caught on the wire of the fence and above it leaned a twisted crab tree laden with fruit, bright green apples, some of them blushing a clear pink on the side which had faced the sun. A great many had fallen into the ditch and had rolled together into a solid mass so that from a distance they showed up very distinctly. What a pity it is that the crab is so sour to the taste. I picked one of the red apples and bit it, surely with that red skin it must be sweet! Yet its juices dried up my mouth, though there was a wild tang about it which was not unpleasant.

Out in the mead, about forty yards from the hedge, grows a may tree. Like the crab it leans at an angle and the ground beneath is bare of grass, rammed hard by the feet of cattle and horses, quite a little hollow sunk below the level of the surrounding sward.

On examination the trunk has a definite gloss on one side and the tough bark is badly worn, polished like an old gunstock from constant friction of rubbing beasts. This tree is a natural 'cow comfort', which is the rustic name for trees and posts used by cattle. Here and there a few wisps of coarse hair are caught in the crevices of the bark and the chaffinches will hunt these out next spring. Horsehair is a favourite nest lining for many birds.

On the hot days the cattle stand for hours at a time beneath the tree, rubbing their hairy flanks against the iron-barked stem. How did this tree grow and survive, out in the open field, why was it not bitten off in its early years by cattle and sheep? A few of its upper leaves are now a beautiful rose red, later all will drop and collect in the hollow beneath and the fieldfares will come for the red berries.

All summer long the wind has whispered in the leaves of the willow, it has rustled the tall poplars yonder and the bright brooklet has chuckled onwards, every hour, every day, every year, on its journey to the remote sea.

What millions of gallons must have flowed away, a whole ocean of water. Whence came it? Surely not from the condensation of the clouds, all those tons and tons of water! There is no high ground about here, no lofty hill which would attract the rain and break the clouds.

Not so long ago the cuckoo's chime was ringing from coppice to hedge and all the meads were white with hawthorn snow; shy warblers swung on the willow wands, timorous moorhens have quested along the boggy margin of the brook, whitethroats have built in the nettle brake by the fence gap. There has been nobody to see, only the clouds have gone over and perhaps a passing shower pattered in the night.

This quiet angle of the meadow was a beautiful place, untidily perfect after Nature's own way. What a jolly time the water voles must have had, plopping in and out among the sturdy sedge swords whose sharp edges can cut the incautious hand! The wild iris have bloomed in their season and no-one has come to gather them; wild animals, little wild animals, have come to drink in the grey before the dawn.

Swallows and martins have come, gathering plaster for their homes built in shed and under eave, walking awkwardly on their puny feathered feet, flying away with wee balls of mud in their bills, twittering happily despite the fact of their mouths being so full.

So, thought I, must there be untold millions of little meadows such as this all over the kingdom where nobody comes near all summer long, save birdnesting boys of a Sunday.

Now the warblers have gone and the leaves are going, the autumn dusk steals down the valley and the sun sinks low.

Whatever man can do so will it always be; this stream will run onwards to the sea, the simple plovers camp on yonder rushy slope. Peace here always and the passionless march of the years will go on.

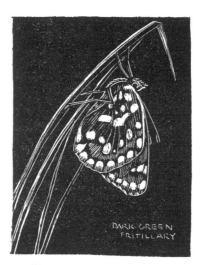

Dark Green Fritillary

CHAPTER V

The River

Chapter V

The Carse has been a happy hunting ground of mine for many years.

This fertile plain, which lies next to the river, is wonderful growing land for crops, and like the Lincolnshire Fens is perhaps the most valuable land in Britain, worth anything up to £100 per acre.

The Carse itself is uninteresting, being merely flat fields with farm steadings and dour buildings, very often with a tall grey silo somewhere near by. It is bounded on its northern side by a range of hills which are not important enough to be considered as mountains, yet are more imposing than a mere rampart of hills. In mid-winter its higher crests are usually powdered with snow and sometimes there are beautiful effects when, looking across the dark earth of the Carse, one sees the setting sun light up that distant range with a faint rosy tinge such as one sees on those little shells on the sea-shore. I know the country well in its many moods; in the late summer time when the vast reed beds along the river are green and gracefully plumed, and the harvest is stooked on the flat fields; rich heavy-headed crops which would do many a midland farmer good to see.

In the evening the curlews flight in from the stubble in

goose-like formations and, strangely enough, making very duck-like sounds when they are close overhead and do not see you.

In the reed beds the mallard flappers are everywhere, and at high tide with the wind in the west, they fly down the edge of the reed beds in a never ending line. Unless one has a good dog however, you will lose nearly all your birds.

Those that fall into the river will be carried away and those that fall into the reed jungles will never be found save by pure chance. These reeds grow to a tremendous height (ten and eleven feet), and it is almost impossible to force a passage through them.

Generations of growth have bedded down into a breast-work of criss-crossed broken reeds through which the new growth thrusts up forming dense pallisades. It takes a good dog to face this cover and find a fallen bird.

The reason for the formation of these reed beds is interesting. Many years ago an effort was made to reclaim the mud flats next to the river, and experts, many of whom were Dutch engineers used to tackling such problems, were called in to deal with the situation.

Long stone breakwaters were built out from the land into the estuary and reeds were planted to bind the mud. Years went by and very soon mud deposits began to form behind and between the breakwaters. Each succeeding tide brought up more mud and sand which, when the tide receded, was caught between the stone walls. The reeds grew and bound the mud together but the process was too slow for man. The breakwaters were no longer kept in good repair, they sank into mud and sand, allowing the full force of the tide to sweep up the river. After a while we, being British and not Dutch, allowed the whole scheme to slide. But still the reeds spread, sending their long tubers out under the mud, throwing up new shoots, growing denser every year. Someone must have had the idea of thatching a barn with some of these tall reeds; perhaps he was a Norfolk man and knew how they stood the weather. Gradually a new industry arose and out of failure something useful was found.

These reeds are as good as Norfolk reeds for thatching and the industry still flourishes. Every autumn the reed cutters get to work and cut large spaces and lanes among the reed jungles. These spaces are excellent places to stand for flighting; the duck and geese are over before they spot you, but a bird hit is most difficult to mark down. In an instant your target tops the reeds, you fire, you see him fall, you hear the crash of the body in the reeds, but unless you have an excellent dog your chances of finding your bird are remote.

It is the winter however which casts a spell, a magic spell for me, upon this 'goose country'. The reeds are no longer green but bleached to a whitish buff, the wind passes over, and they rustle mournfully together, bowing their plumed heads. Yet even in death they do not lose their grace, and many an evening I have watched those slender stems, crowned with a feathery head, etched against the red of a sunset sky, reminding me of an exquisite example of Japanese lacquer work.

In times of peace my annual pilgrimage to some kind friends in the Carse takes place in the New Year, usually in the period of the full moon. This last January 1940, I managed to reach my happy hunting grounds by novel, if expensive, means.

Despite repeated attempts to persuade a half-hearted government to accept my service in the armed forces I found myself still at liberty to hunt the wild geese, possibly for the last time. As I was not able to obtain the necessary petrol for the long journey from the midlands I solved the problem by taking the car by rail to Carlisle and motoring from there. It was an adventure.

H   C.B.B.

The winter of 1940 would have been always memorable for other reasons than the weather, but the frost and snow which arrived just at the time I was going north was unprecedented.

There had been snow before Christmas, nothing very much it is true, but it was the advance guard of what was to come. I remember one moonlight night a few days before I left, standing on my lawn listening to the wild pipes of curlew passing over and, a little later, wild geese. In vain did I search the stars, I could see no flying shapes, yet I knew such things foretold hard weather.

A sharp fall of snow with frost following deterred me from starting, as had been arranged, on the 27th of December. A temporary thaw came a day or two later so I packed my bags, and booked a van for my car from Rugby.

On the day I was to go I awoke to see an unnatural white glare on the bedroom ceiling and on looking out of the window saw the little macrocarpi trees along my garden fence bowed down with crowns of snow. But the ticket was bought, the van booked, and the only thing to do was to hope that the roads would be clear up north.

My wife had prepared my sugar and butter rations, done up in two neat parcels, and at nine thirty p.m. I was ready to start. Busy, my labrador, found that butter and sugar and disposed of it while our backs were turned, and it was with grave misgivings that I locked her in the car and saw her disappear into the van, with the porters' lanterns making swinging patterns on the white platforms, for snow lay deep, and the coloured lights of the signals were like jewels in the dark, ruby, green, and yellow.

The train was crowded. In my first-class carriage were four naval officers, all very weary men. We could find no switch to douse the light in the carriage so I removed the electric bulb and we all slept in the dark. There is something exciting in sleeping in the train. Each bump of the rails seems fraught with romance, and imagination gets busy with the dark wintry countryside without as it wheels past; the little farms set in the lonely hills where people are sleeping; woods, snow-sheeted, where hungry foxes are on the prowl and owls are hooting; the flat riverside fields where the wild duck are feeding and the plover sleeping on the mounded furrow; the wild moorlands, white and open to the sky and stars.

But you, fortunate mortal, are whisked along in warmth and comfort, shut away from the cutting winds, snow, and frosty bleakness of field, wood, and populous town, with only the 'trump trump' of the rail joints to tell you that you are moving at all.

At Crewe a fat and truculent person came into the carriage and loudly demanded a light. A somewhat apologetic ticket collector was summoned and he fumbled for the switch but naturally no light was forthcoming. So he withdrew, still apologetic, and the fat man subsided with muffled curses and heavy breathing on top of the electric light bulb which I had put on the end of the seat. Result, much ill-concealed merriment on the part of my naval fellow travellers and redoubled maledictions on the part of the fat man.

By the beat of the train wheels I knew we were climbing over the Pennines. Before dawn the shepherds would be up watching the light grow over the hills. . . . I should be far away then. Soon the fat man fell asleep and his heavy snores formed a background to my own fitful dreams.

The next thing I knew was a realization that the song of the rails had ceased and there was a profound silence broken only by the clank of milk-cans and the singing of some distant porter. Footsteps echoed down lone platforms. Carlisle! Three in the morning!

I disembarked, leaving the fat man still asleep on the broken electric lamp bulb. Sleepy porters, the rich burr of the Border.

To my surprise there was less snow than in the midlands though it was marrow-freezing cold. I wandered over a maze of platforms to a distant siding where I expected to find the van containing my trusty little car and the anxious Busy. I stamped about in the snow with a porter, our breath making whitish plumes on the Arctic air. Soon a ruby red light came wavering down the line and I recognised the tail of the van advancing through the dark.

Something black scurried over the rails . . . a cat?

'Och no Sirr, a rat, they're swarmin' here, as big as rabbits!' The red eye swam onwards towards us.

'Herre she is Sirr, yon's the van.'

From the dark interior we pushed the car, the door was opened and bolts clanged. Ye Gods! the worst had happened! Busy was dreeing her weird, the ill-digested remains of the butter and sugar rations were all over the back seat, over the gun case, over the rugs and baggage!

Windows and doors were hastily opened and there began the grisly business of cleaning up. The porters had meanwhile vanished so I had to do the job myself. When this was at last completed more or less in a satisfactory manner I looked around for Busy. She meanwhile had disappeared and for an hour I whistled vainly down the goods-yard. Then a draggled and very frightened dog appeared from under a waggon, was beaten soundly and bundled into the car. I had not finished with her yet however.

Having accumulated all the rugs I could find and tucked myself up I soon fell asleep, waking cramped and cold at six thirty a.m. An hotel was suggested and a hot breakfast, and though the sky outside showed no sign of dawn, I began to make a move.

Now on my windscreen I had a defroster which is operated by a switch from the dashboard. The luckless Busy, not content with the havoc already wrought during the hours of darkness, had succeeded in some way or another in turning on this switch with her large black posterior. Result, when I pressed the starter button, a sullen grunt from the engine!

Now here was a nice kettle of fish! I wanted to start by 9 o'clock at the latest but I could not stir the engine and my starting handle was mislaid. I felt as though I was haunted by some ugly little demon who was striving very hard to upset my plans. However my luck had turned, for just outside the yard I found the best garage in Carlisle for the job. The man promised to get the battery fixed by the time I returned from breakfast and so I left Busy in the back of the car, and praying for no more upsets went in search of food.

When I returned (well fortified within) I found all ready. By some means the garage attendant had got the engine running and he assured me that the extra miles I had to go would recharge the battery, so I set off.

There was a thick fog covering the countryside, cars and buses carried lights and speed was reduced to fifteen miles an hour for the first three miles or so. Then, near Canonbie, I saw the road ahead silvered in sunlight and in a moment I had run out of that murky wall and found no trace of fog. The nightmare of a night was forgotten and I settled down to enjoy the lovely sparkling countryside.

The Esk was rimmed with ice floes, on the pine trees frost sparkled, and shaggy sheep bounded up the side of the rough hill slopes.

But this is no record of a journey. I began this chapter with a description of the river and so must hurry thither. Only one thing I must note.

In the Glen the snow was deep on either hand, hanging

from the rocks were huge icicles as thick round as my arm, and the road was sheeted with ice and snow. There was snow too beyond and as I got farther north it deepened. Behind me the sun dipped over the hills and a fog hid the approaches to the distant city.

In the dim lights of the car's headlamps the road pricked fire from millions of ice particles and I had to go carefully round the corners. At last, at seven o'clock that night, I slithered to a standstill opposite my fowling quarters.

It was with a great sense of satisfaction that, after a good supper, I drew my chair up to the fire with Busy's head resting on my knee, and made plans for the morrow.

'Lord Edward' was joining me. He had to come from the wilds of Sutherland and would not be with me until the next day. There was a telegram propped up on the mantelpiece. 'Arriving at——station tomorrow 6.15 can you meet me.'

I must confess that on a wildfowling holiday I must have company, congenial company, it adds much to one's enjoyment. I like to hunt geese alone (and so does 'Lord Edward'), but it is pleasant to talk over one's score around the fireside. We talk about geese and natural history almost exclusively, just as fox hunters will talk about hunting and horses, but this does not mean we have limited interests.

At dawn I would be off to the old hunting grounds at Curlew Bay where in the past I have had many a goose. I wondered then where the geese would be feeding, and speculated on the circumstances of my first shot.

I looked round the room with a loving eye; the same pictures were on the walls, the castle wood outlined against the soft orange sky and the cattle fetlock deep in the water. A bad picture, indeed, as an artist I should say it was rock bottom, yet I have an affection for it and it stirs my imagination. Any moment a bunched skein might rise over those

Goose Country—Dawn

dark trees and be reflected in the water in front of the high-land cattle.

I was up an hour before dawn and found the garage doors frozen. There had been a powdering of snow in the night and I slipped about all over the place in my rubber boots.

The stars were still bright as I went down the rutty lane towards Curlew Bay and the noise of the wheels in the ice of the ruts was like crashing glass. In a few minutes I was going down the cart track between the trees.

Nothing had changed since the year before; on the little pond on the right of the track, under the leaning willow, were the same dim immobile blobs of the Muscovy ducks and I had to use the same persuasion with Busy not to re-trieve them.

My way now led across the orchard between the old twisted apple trees. Dawn was not yet in evidence, the stars were still shining and there was only the faintest trace of grey in the east. I reached the bank overlooking the river and saw the wide expanse of water glimmering between the trunks of the tall beech trees. These trees are very large and fine, and at one place on the bank form quite a little wood.

Bob Kennedy, my wildfowling friend, who lived in a little cottage on the 'Mains', shot a good many pigeon here when the beech mast was ripe, and he had built a hide, quite a roomy affair, cosily thatched with branches under one of the tallest trees.

Only last week I had the sad news that Kennedy had gone. After a long and painful illness he died in the local hospital.

For many years Bob and I had worked together in our wild-goose chasing and I suppose no other man in Britain shot more geese with the shoulder gun. Kennedy's health was ruined in the last war when he had a bad dose of gas;

this may have been the cause of his comparatively early death, for he was by no means an old man.

Besides being a great goose hunter he was a fine naturalist, possessing a deep knowledge of birds, beasts, and fishes. I used to send him butterflies which I caught in my own midland woods; species which he did not find in Scotland. He was also a very good artist and taxidermist. The last time I saw him was one morning in January 1940. I can see him now, coming along the top of the sea wall with his faithful spaniel at his heels. In the bag on his back were two heavy greylag ganders, shot with a clean right and left as the skein came in over the reeds at dawn. I had seen those shots myself, for I was hiding in the reeds two hundred yards below him and had noted the long line of black birds heading straight for him. Two dots had fallen, to be followed a second or two later by the sound of the double reports.

Good old Kennedy, may God rest his soul. I shall miss those friendly chats we used to have round his little cabin fire, and those lonely vigils at dawn and dusk on the wild upland fields waiting for the geese to come in from over the hills.

But to return to my narrative. Even during the winter, pigeons are fond of roosting at this place and one or two flew out as I took the track along the top of the bank.

A slanting path or cart track led down the bank and in a moment or two I was on the level marsh with the reed beds in front of me, which grew in thick belts, high enough to hide most of the river.

The ground close to the bank was slightly soggy, but as I went farther out, the matted reeds and short tide-washed grass were crisp and white.

Wildfowl could now be heard out on the river, mallard quacking and an occasional goose calling. I had not heard the latter sound for twelve months and rejoiced in it.

I now had to walk along the edge of the reed beds and it was difficult to do so without making a noise. Many of the reeds had fallen and matted into barriers which were frozen on top, but soft underneath, and here and there my weight broke through to the ice below. But by moving a step at a time, I could progress without undue disturbance.

Very soon I came to the little bay, a good spot for roosting greylags. I have never quite understood why the 'greys' like this bay so much. Though there are ample reed tubers for them to feed on (the staple diet of the greylag), this also applies to the rest of the coastline. It may be they are seldom disturbed and also in rough weather it is a little haven.

I reached the farthermost edge of the reed bed, and finding a plank half hidden in the reeds, I pulled out my air cushion which I always carry with me, and sat down.

At such times the joy of a pipe is forbidden. The only time I smoke whilst wild fowling is on the evening flight, and even then it is not advisable, for if a duck or goose should suddenly present a shot, and one fires with a pipe between the teeth, it is likely not only to break the pipe but the teeth as well. Though it was a bitter morning I was warm enough in the shelter of the reed beds, and I had on my thick khaki overcoat.

It was still far too dark to see if there were any geese on the muds off the bay, but I heard a good many moving about on the river. Then things became quiet, and all I heard was the wind rustling in the tall reeds.

Very slowly the east began to brighten, showing up the dark lines of the hills on the opposite side of the river, and from an anchored steamer a tiny point of light flickered; inland the farm cocks could be heard crowing. It was the opening day of the salmon fishing and no doubt the light on the river was from a trawler putting down the nets.

Mallard passed over, I could hear their wings but could not see them. Now and again I heard the small stuttering quacks which tell of flighting duck. I was rather astonished a moment later to hear a greylag croak exactly opposite me in the short reeds. From the sound it appeared to be only about thirty yards away, but I knew sound carries a long way over water and in reality he was probably a hundred yards or more out on the muds.

Icebergs on the Estuary

Soon it was light enough to see the goose tracks in the soft wet mud, newly uncovered by the tide. These criss-crossed in all directions and showed that the geese had been feeding during the hours of darkness, in the short reeds all round me. Here and there it was possible to see where a goose had pulled up the reed roots, for there were ragged black holes in the mud.

A tiny black object, which looked more like a rat than anything else, rustled among the short reeds about ten feet away and darted across an open space and then, seeing me, stopped. It was a water rail. These little birds are everywhere in the reed beds and are difficult to flush even with a good dog. When they do fly it is only for a short distance and then they drop again into cover. The high pitched scream is a characteristic sound in the dense reed beds. It stood for some time perfectly motionless save for a slight flirting of the tail. Against the drab tones of the background I must have been almost invisible but it still remained watching me. The open space was about ten feet across but the little chap could not make up his mind to dash over. Once it advanced half way then scuttled back. Then at last it made up its mind to make a dash. Down went its head and it shot over at lightning speed, travelling so fast that its legs were a mere blur. It was followed a second later by its mate. When you see the water rails begin to move you know it is time to press the catch from 'safety', for the geese will be coming very shortly.

Not far away, on the tip of a mud bar, I could see a cluster of black blobs. They were, no doubt, greylags. They were still asleep but as they were against the paling water they were visible to me. For quite a time I fixed my eyes on those black blobs and was quite unable to make up my mind whether they were alive or not. Then, sure enough, I saw one move. It was walking towards the water. The others followed and soon a long string was moving down the mud bar. They slipped into the tide and began to swim away.

On my left I saw the dark bar of the breakwater sticking out into the river, like a black sword blade pointed outwards from the land. Geese began to call all around.

Then a goose called so loudly I almost jumped. By the sound it could not have been more than ten feet from me. But between me and the river edge was a short belt of reeds. I half rose with the gun at the ready but I was not quick enough. With a tremendous 'woosh' the goose rose from behind the reeds and in a moment was hidden against the dark tones of the marsh. I could never have believed that it would be possible to get so close to a sleeping wild goose without being heard or seen, for however carefully one treads in the reeds there is always a certain amount of rustling.

From the direction of the breakwater the cackling was redoubled and a moment later a whole string of greylags hove in sight, hugging the edge of the reed bed and heading directly for me. I squatted down and brought the gun to my shoulder but when they were about sixty yards from me they turned and went leisurely inland.

If I had been only a few yards to my left I should have had a glorious shot. By now it was getting quite light and out in the river I could see long lines of geese on the water swimming down with the tide.

Then I heard more geese approaching and another skein came in on the same line. This time they did not alter course but came straight past me at a range of about forty yards. I was so excited that I missed clean with my first barrel, but steadying up I fired a careful shot with the left and saw the second goose in line throw up its wings and crash to the mud. At the sound of the shot a babel broke out on all sides as all the geese in the river took wing and went inland. For a minute or so the sky was streaked with skeins.

Then I walked across the mud and reeds, sinking in to the calf. I could not see the fallen goose anywhere but I luckily knew that the light was getting stronger every moment and I was sure to find him,—my dog I had left at home for some obscure reason.

Very soon I saw it, almost at my feet, a very fine old bird with its wings spread out like a grey cloak on the tops of the reeds. So closely did it harmonize with its surroundings that I had walked past it several times as my footsteps in the mud clearly showed.

I took him up by the pink paddles and found it was cleanly killed with not a feather out of place.

Grazing Greylags

CHAPTER VI

The Shore Gunner

Chapter VI

Looking back on all the goose hunts I have had in Scotland through the generosity of good friends, I can count many good days which stand out in the memory. Yet it is not always the good days which are the most interesting; there have been many long fruitless stalks and vigils which, though from the point of view of killing geese have been disappointing, yet because of interesting things seen they were outstanding.

When I first set out to put these notes together I made up my mind that there was to be little 'killing' and more of natural history. But as I am a hunter-naturalist, observation and sport go hand in hand. Besides which, I must confess that at the moment I have a bad attack of 'goose fever'. This disease assails me every year at this time, namely in the autumn, and my mind is so full of reminiscences I must recount a few more goose chases before I leave the subject.

All true wildfowlers will know what I mean by 'goose fever'. We all get it, and it is a catching complaint. The symptoms are a craving for the books of Millais and St. John, Col. Hawker and Abel Chapman. Of the four, I like

Col. Hawker the least. Hawker was a butcher and nothing else. We get no hint that the true glamour of the pursuit of wild-fowl appealed to him, or that he was an observant naturalist; he was only interested in big shots at fowl with a punt gun. Sometimes indeed his diary is quite sickening. He seemed to shoot everything, even butterflies. With Hawker shooting was not a sport but a mania. What a relief it is to pick up a book by Chapman, who was a great naturalist in addition to being a skilled wildfowler. Though his style is at times a little verbose and dictatorial I never find him dull and, what is more important, he has always some fresh observation to make. He was, in my opinion, the best type of wildfowler and something of an artist as well.

It is a strange thing to say, but the finest wildfowlers are artists. Why this should be I cannot imagine, as destruction and creation are so opposed to each other, but there it is. Millais was an artist, Peter Scott is an artist—and a very fine one—Frank Southgate was an expert wildfowler and artist, Abel Chapman, already mentioned, and many more. And all the old wildfowlers on the coast, who are really first class men, are artists in their way, like my old friend Bob Kennedy referred to in the last chapter.

We certainly do see some lovely pictures when we are out on the marshes or the hills and we long to perpetuate them in paint and prose. There is no romance in game shooting, especially from stands. I can get little enjoyment out of a grouse drive or a pheasant shoot; organised slaughter is horrible.

I know all this has been said over and over again, but wildfowling is the last really wild sport which can be enjoyed in Britain, with perhaps the exception of deer stalking, of which I have never been fortunate enough to have had experience.

For the uninitiated I must explain the habits of wild geese (the old campaigner can skip these pages).

As every naturalist knows—or should know—wild geese are winter visitors. Only the greylag breeds with us—in the remote highlands of Scotland—though the greylags that haunt the Scottish estuaries are not all home bred birds. Many of them come from the Arctic with the other geese; pink-feet, bernicle, and white-fronted.

They begin to arrive in October, and by the end of November the main bulk have come in. Pink-footed geese arrive earlier than the other species and by the middle of September they will be found on the Yorkshire wolds, feeding on the stubbles and flighting out to the sea at night.

During moonlight periods wild geese feed largely at night but when the nights are dark they roost out on the sand banks and feed during the day.

There are several ways of shooting them; by the punt gun, which is a large calibre gun mounted on a boat, and by the shoulder gun. I have done very little punting and do not like it as much as shooting with the shoulder gun. Both methods require considerable skill, both are equally difficult. As I have said elsewhere, the shooting of the goose is as difficult as the stalking and shooting of the stag; some people say that geese are much harder to shoot.

From early times the goose has been hunted, no other bird seems such good return for powder and shot; he is as much as a man can comfortably carry and is considerably more than one man can eat, even though he be a very hungry hunter.

The greylag is the largest of all the wild geese, an old gander weighing anything up to ten or eleven pounds. Sometimes when one sees them feeding on the stubble it is hard to believe they are not domestic geese. There have been one or two occasions when I have been so mistaken.

I remember once stalking some wild geese which had alighted on a Perthshire farm at dusk. It was a long and very wet stalk as I had to 'belly crawl' over a wide field to where I had seen the birds pitch.

In one corner of the field was a drinking trough, close to the farm yard. My idea was to get up behind this trough and so gain the advantage of some dead ground which would enable me to crawl up to the feeding birds. I managed to get across the field, though it took me a long time and the light was fast failing. When I was within about twenty yards of the trough, two geese walked out from behind it and stood with upraised heads looking at me. I thought they had strayed through the gate just beyond and began to hope that they would not alarm the wild geese out in the next field.

Suddenly one began to give a low croak, uncommonly like that of a wild goose, and to my amazement both birds took three or four steps forward and rose into the air. It was quite a second before I realized what a chance I had missed.

Those geese had walked up behind the trough while I was crawling across the field; that second wasted meant that I had no time to bring the gun to the shoulder and fire.

These 'greys' are curious creatures and year after year will frequent the same meadow and same strip of marsh. Many of the Perthshire fields I know are used by geese every season. They are always to be found in the same corner or stretch of rising ground and will not feed on the adjoining pastures, though to all appearances they are identical.

One such field I will describe. It is small and triangular, bounded on one side by the sea-wall and on another by a burn, the banks of which are thickly grown with alders. In the middle of the meadow the ground is raised and geese alighting in this place are unstalkable. Perhaps this is one of the reasons why they like it so well. I have never seen 'pinks' alight upon it, it is almost exclusively the feeding ground of the greys. They come in off the river at dawn and if undisturbed will feed there all day, sitting down when they are weary and sleeping in the open.

After a day or two someone will get a shot at them and they will forsake the place for a time, but before very long will resort again to the same pasture and the same plateau.

One cannot depend on the 'greys' in the way you can depend on the pinks. They are strangely erratic creatures. Pinks are much more fixed in their habits and will come in force to a certain locality, week after week, for grazing. The greys never seem to go about in such large companies; fifteen to twenty seems to be the average number in a skein. They also keep much more to the river and do not flight out at dawn to distant feeding grounds. They use the meadows and fields within four or five miles of the river, whilst their kinsmen the pinks will take long flights over the hills.

One little marsh I know right on the edge of the river is a favourite resting place for greys during the hours of day-light. At this spot the sea wall is clothed thickly with broom, which forms an excellent 'hideout' for the lurking gunner.

In frosty weather, or on foggy days, they dribble in off the river and pitch among the short reeds just on the edge of the water. One misty afternoon I was hiding up in the whin bushes with my labrador beside me. Curlew had been streaming over, for the tide was flooding.

I could see, far out in the middle of the river, a low bank black with curlew and other fowl, and as the tide rose they came off in twos and threes right over my hide.

I am fond of curlew shooting and have had very many at this place, but as geese were about I did not wish to disturb the latter by shooting.

It was the kind of evening I always like. One never knows what may come your way and the mist adds mystery to everything and colours the passing moment with romance.

All at once there was a sudden outburst of curlew pipes, a lovely chorus. From the far sandbank every bird was up, fully five hundred or so. They came in over the whins and crouching there I could see every detail of the graceful long-nosed birds and the beautiful striations on their breasts and snow-white undertail coverts.

Slowly the tide flooded up over the marsh and little parties of snipe dropped down out of the fog. Mist after warm winter weather usually means frost. Already there were silver ferns on the hanging grass blades by my side. The distant sandbank was hidden by tide and mist. The latter rolled in off the sea and far away I heard the bellow of steamer sirens.

And then I saw six heavy flapping shapes come out of the fog, straight in for the marsh in front of me. They came in boldly without a sound and with apparent lack of their usual caution, pitching right in the edge of the stubbly reeds where they were hidden from me by a low bluff. It was the 'gift' of a stalk. The marsh was only about seventy yards wide at this spot and all I had to do was to crawl across and peep over the knoll.

I began my crawl, pushing my way down through the whins, my hand grasping the collar of the labrador. All went well for thirty yards or so; then Busy's eyes began to bulge and her nose to work. She knew the geese were just over the bank and could wind them. Another yard or two and she began to make little suppressed squeaks in her throat. Her ears were like two question marks. In vain did I hiss at her, threats were of no avail, she only laid back her ears for a moment and gave me a quick sidelong glance.

When I was almost at the bluff she suddenly let out a

squeal of excitement. I gripped her muzzle and in doing so caught her tongue between her teeth. She let out a loud squeal. There was a sudden 'horoosh' from the bank and the greylags took wing, turning their heads sideways to look over their shoulders and giving the low quacking alarm note. I released the dog's collar and got my gun to my shoulder but it was too late. The fog had swallowed them up and a golden chance was lost through an ill-trained dog.

Yet Busy has her uses. She is better than my spaniel at retrieving fallen birds, both in thick cover and from across the muds. The spaniel has such short legs she gets bogged. Busy, with her long and graceful legs, can hop over the rotten mud and she works more by sight. A full grown goose is a big mouthful for a dog, especially a spaniel. Labradors, having the longer leg and bigger mouth, are the ideal wildfowler's dog if they are well trained.

This marsh I have just described is an excellent place for snipe, indeed it is the best on the whole coast. When the tide is at the full they congregate in the short reeds and afford wonderful sport. As soon as the water goes down again they spread about, up and down the marshes, and are not so concentrated.

In very hard weather however the snipe go away and one may walk the whole marsh and never put one up. It is a dangerous little place, as here and there are deep 'guts', eaten out by the action of the tide and half concealed with dead and broken reed. Even when bound in ice and snow, the foot breaks through the crust and if you are not careful you are thrown forwards, the whole weight of the body coming on the shin bone.

Very occasionally one can find a hare at the upper end which has come in off the fields on the other side of the sea wall, and on one occasion I put up a covey of partridges.

There are no high reed beds at this point, they are found lower down.

One word about the reed beds. A young subaltern friend once spent a very bad night in these dense reed forests. As they come well above the head he lost his bearings. There were no stars to guide him and he spent about five hours battling his way in a circle. It is most exhausting work, as I know, for I also have been lost in the same way.

As the old reed growth is about breast high it forms a barrier and the only way to make any progress is backwards. After about half an hour's pushing in this manner, clad in thick wildfowling clothes, sweaters, thigh boots and the like, one is utterly exhausted.

On the whole I have had more fun shooting actually on the marshes than chasing the geese inland. But it sometimes happens that all the geese seem to go away over the hills and the river is empty. There is only one thing to do then and that is to chase them. This may entail motoring many miles to find their feeding grounds. Mild open weather is the best for river hunting; if it comes a very hard frost the tubers—the reed roots of which the geese are so fond—are bound into the mud and they cannot get at them, and they then forsake their old haunts until gentler weather.

Nevertheless I have had some very enjoyable days inland and I will close this chapter with the account of a most successful goose hunt on an inland field.

After a week of mild weather, in which we got several geese, a hard frost set in and the marshes were frozen. All the geese in the river seemed to go away and the night before the frost I saw skein after skein heading away north over the hills. Wherever one looked one could see little black bundles hung in the sky, bundles which con-

The Fowler

stantly changed shape, bunching one moment, attenuated the next.

The following morning not a goose was to be heard or seen, so there was nothing to do but consult our old friend Bob Kennedy. We were at his little cottage bright and early and found him just finishing his breakfast with his spaniel sitting waiting for scraps.

'I know what you've come for,' said Bob, 'no geese on the river, eh?'

'Not a goose, Bob.'

'Ah, that means they'll be awa' over the hills. I know where we'll find 'em, there's only one thing to do. We must chase 'em. It's coming full moon now and they will be feeding at night when the men have left the fields. The best thing for us to do is to go and see the grieve.'

So an hour or two later my friend and I, plus Bob and his spaniel, were speeding up the mountain road. It was a wonderful morning, so wonderful I can see now the pale wintry sunlight flooding the tawny bracken on the hillsides and the white frost on the shadowed banks. We reached the summit of the pass and dropped down the other side.

Once we saw a lovely sight. On our right a humped field of golden brown plough, beyond was a birch wood, the stems silver in the sunlight, and wheeling round and round over the field with their blue shadows under them, was a skein of about fifty pink-footed geese.

Though we were fairly close, not more than a hundred yards or so, the geese ignored us, and with a graceful sweep they all came to rest on the centre of the field. After looking at them for some time we continued on our way. In the fresh light of the morning the country was spread out below us; the far fir woods and scattered plantations, the wide fields and little farms, each with their cluster of conical ricks, and far in the distance more blue mountains on the horizon. In places where the sun had not reached the road, care was necessary, for overnight there had been about an inch of snow on this high ground and the twists and turns were dangerous.

Soon we were down on the flat fertile plain and after several winding roads we eventually drew up opposite the farm. We found the grieve at his lunch (it was eleven o'clock) and he came down the garden to meet us.

He was a man of about five foot eleven with dark hair and a face like an eagle. There was something almost Welsh in his appearance. His fine dark eyes, looking out from beneath bushy brows, reminded me of some hawk or falcon. He had an almost gipsyish, wild look about him. When he talked he looked you straight in the eyes.

'Och yes to be sure the geese were using the fields right enough, there's no mistake aboot that.'

He had seen them the day before, he had heard them all night long, indeed, they had made so much noise they had disturbed his sleep!

'They may be there now, doon on the far field, that's where they come, on the last field on the edge of the farm, near the fir wood.'

We walked down the lane by the big ricks. A bitter wind blew out of the north but it was a morning of glitter and sunlight. Our boots crunched and squeaked on the thin snow covering and cracked hollowly on the ice skins over the cattle pocks. Below the farm the fields sloped away; it was hard to tell which was stubble and which arable, all was hidden under the white covering. Here and there I could see a long potato or swede camp; in one field a lot of sheep were feeding round some hay dumps. But I could see no goose.

To the north the hills stood out sharply against the hard

pale blue sky. Right overhead an aeroplane passed, its wings a transparent yellow against the bright light. It must have been cold work flying up there!

The grieve raised his dark eyes until they fastened on the 'plane.

'Those are the things that skere the geese, they hate 'em. If they are feeding and an aeroplane comes along, up they get and go back to the river.'

I took out my glasses and scanned the fields.

In a distant meadow, close to a hayrick, a hare was sitting up in the sun washing itself, its shadow blue behind it. Beyond I could see the dark fir wood and grey specks floating in front of it, pigeons no doubt.

I lifted the glasses to the hills. The edges were very hard and white against the sky behind. As I watched, a tiny bundle of specks topped the higher ridge. I looked and looked. For some time that little cluster of black dots hung there, in the centre of a V mark between two peaks. Then another rose behind them, another black cluster. They hung in the air like kites. Then it dawned on me what they were; geese, coming off the river! It was hard to believe they were moving at all, but I suddenly sensed that they were driving onwards at a great speed. Through my glasses I was looking at the skein head-on. Now, with a sweep of the binoculars, I saw other clusters, all rising over the ridge, one, two, three, four, five more. It was a wonderful sight. The clear bright morning, the snowclad landscape and the biting air, the blue shadows and the homely smell of the farm. And those rising skeins bearing down upon us over the sunlit valley. A picture to remember always.

As they topped the ridge they dropped, and with set wings came gliding over the fields, wheeling this way and that, now with a gentle wing beat, now with rigid pinions. They were gliding boats, floating smoothly on a gentle current, occasionally dipping an oar to help themselves along. And very faintly I heard their bugling cries, seeming to come to us from an immense distance, wonderfully musical and sweet.

As they drew nearer they ceased to move their wings and wheeled round in long lines, gliding lower and lower over the snow. Then a clump of trees hid them from view and we thought they were down, but no, in a second they re-appeared, wings beating slowly now, circling over a distant meadow. For some reason however they did not alight. Perhaps there were men in the field or it may have been another aeroplane which made its appearance, taking advantage of the lovely flying weather. The skeins now began to climb again, some going away westwards and the others turning and heading back for the hills.

'They will no feed the noo,' said the grieve, 'there's some one down there nae doot. They'll be back tonight though. If ye were to come ye might get a shot.'

So we went back over the hills and resolved to try for them when the moon rose.

At four o'clock in the evening we were back again. The sun was setting behind the fir wood, a rose red globe, magnified by the evening mists; above, the sky was a pale green and in this light the snow seemed a deep violet. Bob Kennedy had his dog with him so I left Busy in the car, whining piteously with her front paws on the back of the driver's seat.

It was a long walk down to the last field. On the way we passed a multitude of green goose droppings on the snow and a maze of criss-cross paddle marks. There was no doubt that the gaggles had been there the night before and I was all for staying in that place, but Bob knew better and said we should get more shots in the field beyond.

When we got there, perspiring despite the bitter night for we had come well wrapped up, I was inclined to agree with him. I had never seen such a mass of droppings and webbed footmarks. They were all over the centre of the field and here and there were little piles of dung where the geese, fed to repletion, had sat down and gone to sleep.

We spread out at intervals of about sixty yards, lying down on the snow at full length. I felt very conspicuous, but Kennedy swore that the geese would come in to us as they had not been disturbed.

By this time the 'red eye of day' had dipped down behind the firs, leaving a wonderful sky of green and gold in the west. There was all the promise of a still, clear, frosty night.

To the east the moon was already getting up, full and pale yellow. It would not be long before the geese would come, for the grieve had told us up at the farm that they had not been back during the day. The dark blobs of Kennedy and Charles (my shooting comrade) seemed very black against the snow. Behind Kennedy was another dark spot, the spaniel.

Not very far away was a stream, half frozen; as it grew darker I heard a mallard pass over and alight in the bed of the burn. It would have been a good stalk but we were out for nobler game.

Lying there, looking up at the sky, I could see the trembling stars brightening every moment. Over the hills the moon grew brighter also as she climbed the sky. The cold grew more intense, the gun-barrels seemed almost to sear the fingers. I could feel my outer skin of garments cold also, though I was warm enough within, for we had all had a tot of rum before we started.

One or two plover flew overhead, they must have seen us on the white background for they called as they passed, a very lonely little sound.

Without any warning I suddenly heard a goose call, quite close. I had been scanning the sky over the mountains and

K   C.B.B.

had seen nothing. I could see nothing now though I looked about on all sides.

Then I saw a woolly blur against the stars. It was passing to the right of us and circling round. We lay still, hoping it would come within gunshot, but it passed away, still calling, towards the farm. I was willing to bet then that it had pitched on the other field where we had seen so much goose 'sign'. For a long time nothing happened.

By now the sun had long gone and the moonlight was flooding the field. It seemed as light as day. I was sure that the goose had seen us and in this conjecture I was probably right. Wild geese have sharp eyes and we must have been pretty conspicuous against the snowy field.

Far away, in the fir woods, I heard the owls hooting and once, the bark of a fox. And then the moonlight dimmed. Clouds, with astonishing rapidity, came flocking over the hills. Our shadows on the snow dwindled and vanished; instead of the clear moonlight everything became misty and obscure. Was it rain on the way? Surely not for it was freezing hard. Something brushed my ear, then another, and there were faint tickings against my 'mac'. It was snow.

Still we lay, even though the flakes thickened and the moon was a mere luminosity behind the banks of cloud.

Kennedy and Charles appeared no longer as black blobs. They were as white as the field.

There was no feeling in my limbs and my fingers ached. I must get up and stretch my legs. Apparently Charles felt the same, for when I next looked that way he was up and walking about. After a while Kennedy got up too and we met and talked. 'They'll be here any moment now,' said Kennedy. 'This snow is just what we want.' We talked a while and the flask was passed round. Then we went back to our places and sat down again.

I looked at my wrist watch. It was after eight o'clock. If the geese were coming they should be on their way. Then I felt that tingling sensation of expectation. From over the hills I heard a faint clamour. It was the geese in full cry. I lay full length and made sure the catch was pulled from safety. Strange as it may seem I have been often caught in this way and missed a good chance through overlooking this simple fact.

The noise grew. I sensed that towards us, from across the valley, a mighty host was heading in our direction. Louder, louder, and still no sight of them. Then I could hear, in addition to the calling geese the swish of their wings. When you can hear that sound you know that they are getting nicely in range. Then I saw them, indeed the whole sky seemed a moving mass or carpet of black spots. They were coming on set wings. Geese always glide in to their feeding grounds. There was no doubt that they were within range, they could not be more than forty feet up. There should have been no question of missing. It seemed unbelievable that these great birds, which we had seen so often from afar, were really so close, right overhead. There were so many that it was difficult to choose one's target. I was just swinging nicely on to mine when four reports rang out to right and left of me.

The dark spots shot upwards as I fired at one bird on the right. It fell to my shot. At the same time two heavy thumps close behind me told of success. At such times things 'happen very quickly'. It is the same with all tense and exciting moments in life.

I was just going to run across the snow and get my goose when I heard again the clamour of more geese heading in for us. So I lay where I was and slipped another cartridge in the right barrel. My fingers were so numbed with cold and shaking with excitement that I could hardly push it home. Again I saw a gliding mass of shapes heading in for us. But instead of passing over, they all lifted their wings and pitched on the field in front. I could not judge the range, for as soon as they had landed they were invisible.

Then I heard Kennedy's dog rushing out on my left. The geese were still on the ground. I then heard the 'lift' of forty or so wings and I fired both barrels 'into the brown'. It was perhaps an unsporting shot but I was so excited I did not know what I was doing.

My shots were followed by a bump however, and the dog went back to Kennedy with my goose. The latter was swearing. 'Why the hell did you want to fire, I was sending the dog out to put them up.'

As however I knew the geese would turn downwind I judged I had done the right thing.

I am not going to recount in detail the rest of that flight. Suffice it to say that when they stopped coming the snow was littered with geese. In the dusky half darkness they might have been sacks scattered on the snow.

Fourteen was the total bag when we stumbled round counting them, fourteen pinkfeet as fat as butter.

It was indeed a load which we carried back to the farm, a load worth the bottle of whisky (pre-war price) which we presented to the grieve.

Every one of those geese was used. We sent most of them away next day to friends in the South and the one I kept for myself was the best I have ever tasted.

Wild geese should be hung for over a fortnight and then cooked like a domestic goose, stuffed with onions and sage. To my mind the flavour of the meat is far superior to the domestic goose. They are not so 'fat', and the flesh, when well hung, looks not unlike beef.

Many people have told me that they do not like the flavour of wild geese. This is because they have not had them properly cooked. The mistake that so many make is eating them too soon. A wild goose hung for a week is as tough as leather.

The Irish are said to bury a wild goose for a month before eating it, but I cannot recommend this!

Labrador with Greylag Goose

CHAPTER VII

Wild Geese in Skein

Chapter VII

The goose hunt I have just described was the last really good night I had with Kennedy; we had other 'goose chases' but never again, whilst I was working with him, did we really 'get in amongst them'. And thinking things over I am not sure that I want to kill so many geese again in one night. Our bag was small compared to some and came nowhere near a record. I know of some huge bags made in a single night's shooting on the East Coast; such slaughter is sicken-ing. Wild geese are such noble creatures. Think of their hardihood. On the wild winter nights, when the great winds are up and out, and the rain drives like steel knives hori-zontally over the flats, the geese do not shelter like the other animals. Men huddle indoors, cattle are in the shelter of barns and walls, even other birds such as thrushes and blackbirds find some sort of cover. The ducks seek out some sheltered bank or pool set in the hills, every living creature seems to creep into some hole or cranny. But these splendid birds face out the stormy nights, head into wind, unafraid, hardy as old thorn trees.

They are well prepared to face inclement weather. Part

the feathers on a goose's breast and underneath you will find the snuggest set of winter woollies you could devise, a close and felted covering of down. The outer feathers are well waterproofed and the wet simply rolls off them in beads. And though wild geese are so cunning and wary, sometimes they seem to be pathetically trusting. If they are allowed to feed undisturbed for any length of time they soon begin to lose their instinctive fear of the two-legged animal. They will feed close to busy highways, and in Lincolnshire I have frequently seen them within gunshot of a road.

But never, under any circumstances, have I found them 'silly' on the actual coast. You may shoot a score of geese inland on their feeding grounds to two shot on the marshes. And it is on the marshes I prefer to chase them every time.

It would be interesting to know how many geese Bob Kennedy shot in his lifetime. As far as I know he never kept a record but the numbers must have run into thousands. He was a true hunter and never wasted a shot, or what is more important, a bird. Kennedy would no more dream of shooting a gull than he would his dog. It is only the cad who shoots gulls (save the devilish black-back) and the little fair waders—the dunlins and the stints—on the coast. Knot are fair game and so are golden plover, for both species are excellent eating and golden plover take a deal of shooting.

It will seem strange to go over those old haunts again and find no Kennedy. Of all the characters of the coast he was, I think, the most interesting man I have met. He was an expert taxidermist and frequently mounted specimens for local schools and museums. On the walls of his little cabin he had many paintings of wildfowl, excellently done and, considering he had had no lessons, he was quite a genius.

I was able to give him a few tips with his oil paintings and send him specimens of natural history from time to time.

He had that look in his eyes one only sees in sailormen and airmen, bright blue eyes, half screwed up, as though to protect them from the driving rain.

Poor fellow, I understand that two days before he died he asked to be allowed to smell the earth he loved so well, that sweet rich scent of earth which meant so much to him.

A favourite haunt of mine in my early days of wildfowling used to be the country around Montrose. This was a grand centre for goose hunting and the 'Basin' a good place for all kinds of wildfowl. I believe now that the hateful aeroplane has done much to ruin the shooting, for geese and duck seem unable to become familiar with them.

I am speaking of the days before the present war when flying was not so general.

A river runs into the Basin on its western side and I remember hooking my first salmon there just below the Brig o' Dun. One afternoon in early September I was trout fishing. There was a good run of sea trout coming up, and the rod below me was getting some good sport, though I could not connect with a single fish.

Suddenly a fine salmon jumped at a bend of the river some fifty yards below me and I resolved to try for him. I put on a large red and silver fly I had bought in Austria. It was a gaudy creature, not unlike an outsize in Silver Doctors. I never thought for a moment I should connect, it was more out of fisherman's boredom than anything else, for my tackle was quite unfitted to try conclusions with so royal and massive a fish.

I began to flog the water where he had jumped and he actually leapt again, close to my fly. Two fishermen came along the bank and stood watching me for a while.

'Och but you'll never catch yon fush while he's jumping like that,' said one of them.

'He's a bonnie fush though, a twenty pounder by the looks of him.' And they went on their way.

I kept on flogging the water and was just on the point of giving up when the rod was nearly wrenched from my hands. For a moment I could not realize what had happened.

The reel whizzed and the rod-point bent until the tip touched the water. The river at this point is about thirty yards wide and opposite to me was a shingle bank. The salmon charged across and beached himself, a magnificent creature like a silver torpedo. He did not remain there more than a split second. With a mighty fillip he was back again and went away down the river, taking out the line at such a pace that the reel vibrated and shuddered.

I was in an awkward position. Behind me was a steep bank and I could not clamber up it in time. The fish was travelling at a great pace and soon all my line would be gone. I must get up the bank at all costs. I turned round, at the same time shouting to another angler who was fishing round the next bend. He threw down his rod and came gallantly to my assistance. Just at that moment however there came a slackening of the line and my heart sank. He was off. On looking at the reel I saw that there was still about fifteen yards on the drum but the salmon had run off the line until he had come to a kink on the reel. I had neglected to wind the line properly.

In the early autumn I have had some good fun on the marshes at the head of the Basin. Teal were common and an occasional mallard found its way into the bag, but in September the geese had not arrived.

In January however I have had some good sport at geese and I can recollect many morning flights on the turf wall at the western end. A good many wigeon frequent the muds during the night, flying out to sea just as it begins to get light.

How well I came to know that path to the Basin, along by the river below the Brig o' Dun. It seemed a long way in the darkness before dawn, with the rushing river glimmering pale and ghostly on my right. At the end of the path is a rough bit of marsh and very often there was a mallard or two here, sitting on a shallow tidal pool under the bank.

It was necessary to wade across this water to reach the sea bank and marsh beyond, which bordered on the Basin. I used to so time my tramp that the dawn was just beginning to flush in the east as I crossed the ford.

Sometimes the geese would be sitting on the edge of the water, within range of the bank, and sometimes they roosted out on the mid banks in the middle of the Basin.

I remember one morning, crawling across the marsh on the other side of the ford. I knew the geese were close for I could hear them calling.

The lights of Montrose were dancing over the water (it was in those far off pre-blackout days) and in their wavering reflections I could see a line of dark blobs sitting on the edge of the tide. Closer in was another dark object which I guessed was a goose and I decided to shoot him sitting. Taking careful aim I fired and the line of geese arose with a loud clamour. The object I had fired at remained. It was a bush, a just penalty for taking an unsporting shot!

As the light grew, parties of geese could always be seen, every morning, going out to the fields and hills.

Montrose is a good spot for a week's wildfowling and is (or was) far more productive than the larger estuaries. Moreover there was a good hotel in the town, amazingly cheap and with every comfort. And in those days, I am speaking of the years preceding the present war, it was by no means overshot. I do not think I ever met a fellow fowler there all the time I hunted this locality.

Though during September I never saw geese 'using' the Basin I had the best sport in the marshes at the head of it during that month. There were plenty of mallard and teal, and an odd snipe or two; even partridges were tolerably common. They came in off the fields next door. And when I got tired of shooting I could take up my fly rod and catch a good breakfast of sea trout. The most vivid memory I have of Montrose is rather an amusing one.

I had gone up a day or two after Xmas with another man who was a keen wildfowler. I did not know him very well, and though we got on together, our tastes did not always seem to be similar. For one thing he was extremely fond of gin (a drink I am also partial to but cannot afford) and the quantity he managed to dispose of was astonishing. As he was a rich man he could afford to have as many drinks as he wished. On New Year's Eve he went out on the spree with several of the wild lads of the town and at one in the morning he found himself on Montrose bridge.

He managed somehow or another to find his way back to our hotel, but as everyone was in a deep sleep (the results of Hogmanay) he could make no one hear. For hours he stood and rang the bell, in vain did he batter on the door, it was all useless. And so, slightly more sober, he returned to Montrose bridge, and spent the rest of his night there, and a grisly vigil it must have been as it was a night of bitter cold.

Meanwhile I was sleeping peacefully in my warm bed, only waking once to the sounds of distant revelry out in the square where all the town populace was gathered to see the New Year in.

Next morning at dawn I was out on the Basin stalking the geese and to give him his due so was Peter, despite his frigid night and thick head.

A Devon Lane

The Scotch are a wonderful people. On the surface they are dour and careful, but on Hogmanay night they belong to a different race, they are even continental.

I have memories of many Hogmanays in Scotland and the finest still stands out in my mind; a moonlit night on a Perthshire field, waiting for some geese to come. By eleven thirty they had not arrived. The next day was Sunday and it 'isn't done' to shoot on the 'Sawbath' in Scotland.

At a quarter to twelve I heard the first skeins coming, and lying full length on the field and looking up at the filmy clouds drifting over the moon, I saw the black arrow-head skeins coming over. The gun was lifted and swung (you can swing and follow through quite well when lying on your back) and I saw a dark spot growing larger and larger as it fell headlong to the ground. By mid-night four geese lay all around me, a fitting finish to the old year.

It is difficult to shoot geese on clear moonlight nights as they are invisible unless they are very low. But with a light filmy cloud partially covering the moon you can see them very clearly, even if they are 'well up'.

Before taking leave of the 'goose country' I must say a few more words about it.

I have so many recollections of wonderful times there, due in a great measure to the generous and kindly Scotch. I have spent long days out on the fields, waiting behind a hay screen placed against a fence, and with stuffed decoys out in front, in the hope of shooting the geese on their feeding grounds, and if not shooting them, just watching them.

I have never done any good whatever with decoys, though others have been singularly successful. It may be because I am not acquainted with all the subtle tricks resorted to by the professional fowler. I have lugged hides and decoys for many a sticky ploughed mile on those Northern fields, stumbling along in the pitch darkness burdened with

L   C.B.B.

gear, anxious to reach the feeding places before the geese came in.

But they never seemed to come to the decoys, however cunningly they were placed. Only once, when I was with Kennedy, did a goose come near us and this bird Kennedy shot at an amazing range. It was the longest shot I have ever seen made at a goose, yet Kennedy brought it off. Incidentally he never used any shot larger than ones or twos, and usually shot with fours.

But even if the geese did not alight on your field, it was a grand sight to see the great skeins go out from the river against a stormy dawn sky. Greylags and pinkfeet, the latter easily recognisable by their high squeaking voices, may be seen passing high towards the hills, grey chevrons and wavering lines which seem to move with such slow and flagging wing beats, yet to quickly pass from sight.

There is not the big morning flight such as may be witnessed on the Wash. There I have seen the sky absolutely black with geese soon after dawn, coming off the sea in skein after skein.

Along the foot of the sea bank, close to the tall reeds, woodcock may often be found. Bob Kennedy shot seven in one afternoon. The strangest bird he had ever shot in the marshes was a capercailzie, and the rarest bird he had seen, a spotted crake. It would not surprise me in the least if spotted crakes do not breed in these river reeds. It is a shy and secretive little creature and might easily be confused with a water rail.

Whilst walking along the foot of the sea bank last year, not very far from Kennedy's house, I flushed a woodcock. It flew away from me over the reeds and my big eight bore brought it down at extreme range. It fell in the short reed stubbles and for an hour I searched for it, eventually remembering that my labrador was in the car. I walked a mile to fetch her, set her on the line, and after about five minutes she brought it to me. Busy, for all her faults, has a lovely mouth and frequently brings me waterfowl and baby birds with not a mark upon them. When released they fly away unharmed.

The same evening I had the woodcock I made a beautiful shot at the geese.

All day the weather had been frosty. I had been out on the fields 'decoying' with the usual ill luck.

As the sun went down behind the long avenue of oaks along the sea wall I walked up the marshes on the chance of a duck. Even around the little springs the ground was frozen and one could walk on hummocks of solid opaque ice.

All at once I heard greylags cackling, and turning I saw a skein coming in from the fields. When I first saw them they were behind the trees, so I turned and ran for all I was worth to get under the sea bank. By a great stroke of luck I managed it, and just gained the foot of the wall before the leader, a grey old gander, topped the trees. The single eight bore swung up and the huge goose came crashing down on the ice. He was the biggest grey I have yet shot and weighed over ten pounds. He also had the black barring on the breast which always denotes an old bird. I have also seen a greylag and a pink with so much white on the head, round the base of the bill, that they might have been mistaken for white-fronted geese.

I have never seen or shot the latter, as they do not frequent the coastal marshes where I have done most of my shooting. It is however a very beautiful goose and is more prettily marked than the grey or pink.

Of all the geese the bernicle is the most striking, but not the most attractive, for its size suggests a duck more than a goose. Nevertheless I have had some very exciting times in pursuit of bernicles on the Solway Firth.

I have described some of these barnicle (or bernicle) hunts in an earlier book—the *Sportsman's Bedside Book*— but I have had other hunts since then.

Before I have done with the shooting and hunting of geese I will describe one particularly good night I had during the winter of 1939.

The habits of bernicle geese are different from those of the grey geese. They rarely come inland and must be hunted on the extensive grass marshes where they graze. They will not feed on inland pastures, save very rarely. I have a record of a number seen on the golf links by Berwick, but this must have been unusual.

In appearance they are strikingly marked, with velvety black heads and necks, soft grey backs barred with black, barred flanks, and snow-white undertail coverts and white rumps. They are the smallest of all the geese, and some say, the least wary. I cannot endorse the latter statement, though this may be because I have always hunted them in a locality where they are greatly persecuted.

During the period of the full moon bernicles feed at night and sleep during the day. This is the best time to chase them, as it is possible to stalk them under cover of the tidal channels. There is however a considerable risk to the gunner on this part of the coast if he is unfamiliar with the marshes, and in places the sand is very treacherous.

I had with me a local, who was familiar with the locality, a big 'braw' Scotsman whom I will call Tommy.

Tommy is a well-known character in the little village where I stay when I am shooting on the Solway Firth. Sometimes he is to be found standing on the old wharf where the coasters unload their cargoes, smoking his pipe and passing the time of day with the crews. During the winter he never seems to have much to do, but during the salmon fishing season he is absent for weeks at a time, and some say that he makes enough during the season to keep him for the rest of the year.

On the night in question he and I started off from the village just as the moon was rising, tramping down the coast road until we came to the cart track that led to the marshes. It was a perfect night, with hardly a breath of wind and just enough cloud to make accurate shooting possible.

The trees on either side cast lacing black shadows across the road and here and there, through a gap in the whins, we could see the silver line of the moonlit estuary and the inky black line of the marshes stretching on either side for miles.

For some days past the bernicles had been using a small triangular section of marsh right out on the tide line. It was cut off from the main marsh by tidal gulleys and when the tide was at flood it became an island. It was therefore necessary to crosss the gulley at low water, shoot the geese (if they were there), and be back across the gulley before you were cut off.

When we reached the lane we stopped to listen. The night was so silent that sounds carried an immense distance and it was not long before we could hear, far out on the tide line, the musical murmur of feeding bernicles.

These geese, when they are alone and think themselves safe, keep up a continuous murmur, something between a twitter and a coo. It is a beautiful sound; indeed, when one has stalked them and managed to get within fifty yards or so, the noise is almost deafening, not unlike hundreds of doves softly cooing in a dovecot.

Now and again they suddenly fall silent as though listening for the approach of an enemy. At these times it is wise to remain perfectly still, for it means that the geese are actually on the watch.

'They're there Sirr, nae doot o' that. We must gang quiet doon the gutter if we are to get a shot,' said Tommy in a whisper. We set off down the 'gutter', Tommy leading, his huge black doubled-up figure creeping in front down the silvery path of the moonlit 'runnel', his big boots squelching in the mud.

We progressed in this fashion for two hundred yards or so, pausing now and again for a 'breather'.

We were getting nearer to the feeding geese for the cooing chorus became noticeably louder. But the sound has a ventriloquistic quality about it, one moment appearing to come from the right, and another from the left. We stopped for a counsel of war. Tommy swore that the bernicles were just over the 'brew' as he called it, the slight shelf which is formed by the action of the tides. He did not think they were actually on the island. But as I had been over the ground the day before, in daylight, I had noted the excessive goose sign all over the short grass of the island.

I peered seawards in the dim moonlight, my eyes almost dazzled by the glitter of the moon's rays on the water. Millions of little waders were feeding on the tide's edge. They, like the bernicles, keep up a continuous twittering concert as they feed. It is a wonderful sound and always reminds me of a flock of starlings on a bright frosty morning. Ever and again the host would rise with quite a thunder of wings and all would be silent. Tiny specks could be seen as the flocks wheeled over the sands to settle again higher up the coast, where the same musical murmur would begin again.

It is hard to put into words the magic of a moonlight night on a big estuary. Though all is so still and peaceful the birds are awake and as active as though it were broad day. Few people realize that wildfowl are just as busy, even more so, on a moonlight night, than during the day.

Snipe, geese and duck, plover and curlew, all have no thought for sleep. This is their real day when they may feed unmolested by mankind. The hawks which prey upon them are asleep, it is one grand holiday. Far away I could see the lights of Silloth dancing like golden midges across the water. Always I see those fairy lamps a-dancing wherever I go on the wild marshes. I have seen them on the Wash, on Cromarty Firth, at Montrose basin, and the Dee.

Ah me! those quiet days of peace, what would we not give to have them back again. There was no terror then in the noble dignity of heaven, no sinister pulsing throb of a German bomber up among the stars, no distant sullen bump of high explosive. Peace, peace indeed, one great calm tide of peace, of stars, moonlight and silver sea.

In the distance I could see the pale curves of the wide gulley that separated us from the island, and as I watched I saw a dark shape come down out of the shadow of the opposite 'brew' and swim across the water, followed by another and yet another as a whole string of bernicles came down off the island grass to join others on our side. Jimmy had been right, the 'bernies' were under our bank. It seemed a wonderful stalk, an absolute gift. Yet a moment later our hopes were dashed, for without apparent cause the whole gaggle lifted and went across on to the island. They did not go right away however, for we heard them pitch again on the short grass. There was a leaning pole on the island, a tidemarker. Its reflection was thrown by the moon's rays upon the water.

'We must cross the gulley,' whispered Tommy. And my heart sank.

One thing I dread is crossing these channels at night. But I had confidence in Tommy and he went manfully in, holding his gun high. 'Keep movin' Sirr,' he tossed across his shoulder, 'keep movin' for its a wee bit soft.'

Tommy was half-way over before I saw him begin to flounder. He reminded me of a great bull caught in a bog. His fifteen stone is no joke in a quicksand. He tried to turn but sank deeper in the beastly stuff. He leant forward and nearly fell and my throat went dry as he struggled to reach the bank.

I do not know how he ever got free. When I joined him later (I found a hard bottom on the right of him) the beads of perspiration on his forehead were glistening in the moonlight and he was blowing like a whale.

'Ah but it was soft just there. I thought I should have to roll out.'

It would not be the first time. When Tommy gets into a bad place he lies down in the 'quick' and rolls himself out, a feat which takes more than a little nerve.

It was at this spot that a tragedy happened a year or two previously. Tommy told me about it as he got his wind. An amateur fowler was bogged here and had lost his head. He sank deeper as he struggled and no one answered but the gulls. It was a night like this and nobody within miles.

His hoarse screams of terror were heard however by the fishermen in the distant village and they came with straw and ropes. By then the hapless man had sunk to his shoulders. When they got him out his reason had gone.

Once again on firm ground we debated what to do. In the back of my mind was the horrid thought that the channel would have to be re-crossed again before the tide came in.

Where were the geese? We lay down on the grass and listened for half an hour but not a sound did we hear beyond the piping of the sea pies. These birds began to pass up the sands, whistling hysterically, which is a sign that the tide is on the turn. Far out over the flats I heard the hiss and murmur of the advancing lip of water.

The sound of the incoming Solway tide is an awesome sound if you are out on the flats alone. It comes in at such a pace and cuts you off if you are not wary.

And then I heard the faint yelping of the bernicle pack sweeping down towards us. For some time they were invisible and then, on my left, I saw a mass of silvery white flanks passing over the merse. We dropped like pointers and waited. The geese swept by at thirty yards and we both rose on a knee and, for a second, two gleaming barrels swung with the geese. At the double reports we heard heavy thuds.

And when we walked over we found three geese were down. It was truly a great night, worthy to rank with the night on the northern field when Kennedy, Charles, and I shot the pinks in the snow.

Leaping Salmon

CHAPTER VIII

Frog

Chapter VIII

People have told me over and over again that it is quite inexplicable that a man like myself, who is so in love with nature and wild life, can find pleasure in shooting. I can only answer that, like other hunter-naturalists, I have the hunting instinct very strongly and am never so happy as when I am out in the woods and the fields with a gun under my arm. One of the greatest nature writers of all time, Richard Jeffries, said that he could wish for nothing better than to walk through the woods and fields of England with an old wheel-lock gun. Yet of all men, Richard Jeffries appreciated the wonders of wild nature's ways and his thoughts are the most noble and splendid of all natural history writers.

The truth is, that by way of the gun, one can come to learn many of the secrets of nature and at the same time you are under the open sky at all seasons of the year. Maybe the hunting instinct is a base one and yet it is very natural and perhaps, morally, the least harmful. But like Jeffries I feel that most shooting these days is too easy; with the old flint-lock guns it must have been greater fun and I for one am sorry those days have gone for ever.

I am not trying to make out a case for myself. The reader must take me as I am. If he hates me because I shoot birds and beasts—well, I can see his point of view, I hate myself sometimes. Yet I do not shoot for the joy of killing or I would shoot the waders and sea-pies on the coast and the beautiful sheldrakes. I never shoot a bird which is not edible. The stalking, shooting, and killing of a goose (and I may add, the eating of him) is a pleasurable business to me. There it is, you must take me as I am or throw this book into the fire!

There have been many books, yes, whole books, written on the making of gardens. I do not pretend to be a gardener, but I have worked (though I say it myself) a miracle with my own little patch.

When I came to my present house I found a small, weed-grown oblong of ground fourteen yards by thirty-two. Here and there amongst the nettles, a few faded cabbages were apparent, and the whole little plot did not appear worth bothering about. On the left side was a low wall, three feet high, topped by an iron fence. This side looked out on a pleasant meadow dotted with tall elms. On the right side was a hideous iron fence and over it my next door neigh-bour's garden.

As I had always been used to large gardens and grounds in my old home I was filled with grey melancholy. How could I ever make this miserable allotment a thing of beauty? I began to scheme what I should do, basing my plans on an actual bit of Scottish scenery I had in mind.

First I must have water, running water, better still, a

burn; I must have trees, ferns, and that hideous fence must be hidden from sight. There was no spring to convert into a waterfall but I soon made one. At the house end of the garden there is a little green lawn. French windows open out upon it. This was a good start. I like French windows overlooking a garden. There was another good point. On the far side of the lawn there was a sloping earth bank and the garden behind was on a higher level, about four feet above the lawn. Accordingly I laid my plans. The first thing to be done was to hide the iron fence on the right. I bought ten yew trees, fifty years old, seven feet high and well bushed; these were planted in November against the iron fence, and other small yews were also planted in the gaps between each tree; this completely hid the fence.

The weedy ground was dug over, levelled, and sown down with grass. A flagged path was made up the centre, with five stone steps down the bank to the lawn before the windows. On the left side of the garden, overlooking the field, I planted that fine standby (though slightly suburban), privet. This is going ahead well and has already hidden the fence, though I do not intend it to be too high as the view is a pleasant one.

At the far end of the upper lawn, I planted twelve birch trees, interspersed with Scotch fir and larch. My friends tell me that in a year or two it will be an impenetrable wood, the more flippant suggest pheasant rearing, but these people are the unimaginative ones. Between the birch trees I put in snowdrops, drifts of them, and at the back, against the far wall, daffodils. On the right side of the flagged path I made a long narrow bed which in spring is a blaze of wallflowers and in summer a coloured carpet of antirrhinums.

Now I come to the most interesting bit of the transformation. The sloping bank I made into a rockery, a real rockery with big blocks of local stone. Between the stones I put in fern roots to get the natural effect, and four more birches, older trees which have the beautiful silvery stems. I was lucky in these trees, which came from Wood and Ingram of Huntingdon; they are really lovely birches with an almost golden flush on the bark and very black branches which show up so well against the silvery white bark.

At the top of the bank I made a small pool (in cement) and from it brought my carefully designed 'burn', with three good waterfalls, to the main pool which was dug on the lower lawn just in front of the French windows. This is a good sized affair, nine yards long by four wide (at its broadest point) and three and a half feet deep at the left-hand end. I brought the turf right up to the edge so as to hide the concrete as much as possible. Then, against the house, I made a little shelter for the electric motor, which I sank below the level of the path, and roofed with a stone slab.

An intake pipe was passed from the pool to the pump and another delivery pipe to the upper pool on top of the bank. After some thought I decided I must have a fountain, though it somewhat detracts from the natural appearance of the burn. This diminutive motor uses very little current, less than one electric light point in the house. A turn of the switch indoors and the burn comes cascading down the rocks, falling into the pool at the bottom with a most pleasant sound.

The silver birches are reflected in the water and so (in summer) are the green arching fronds of the ferns. At the right-hand end of the main pool I have planted a red willow bush. The first thing one sees on rounding the corner of the house is this little pool with the cascade, and the reflections of the red and silver stems wavering in the ripples. I planted a water lily at the deep end and installed a family of goldfish. As the water is well aerated it is never foul and opaque, always crystal clear.

My Garden

M   C.B.B.

Dividing the rockery from the upper lawn is a low stone wall planted with aubretia, and round the lower big pool I have pricked in about two hundred snowdrop bulbs. The result may be seen in the accompanying illustration, which I swear is a faithful picture of this transformation scene. I am so pleased with the result that I am willing to offer my services (at a fee!) to any reader who wishes to have a similar natural scene before his windows.

One result of this water garden is that the birds flock to it. All day long there is always a bird or two bathing by the little waterfalls and when I turn the water on they seem to arrive from nowhere. There is a little robin which amuses me greatly. This little red waistcoated goblin builds every year somewhere in the garden but I have never found the nest. As I flatter myself that I am pretty expert at finding nests I take my hat off to him. His most astounding feat is bathing late at night. Sometimes in the autumn dusk I see violent splashings in the upper pool and there he is taking a bath. How he ever manages to get dry is a complete mystery to me. No other bird will ever bathe after sundown.

Sometimes a rowdy flock of starlings descends upon the pool. They all crowd into the tiny basin below the last waterfall, filling it to the brim so that most of the water is ejected. Then there is such a glitter of water drops and flashing stars (for the full plumed male is a lovely bird), such a chattering and a bustle, one gets the notion that they are a crowd of rather vulgar gnomes.

Birds are not the only travellers who call at this green oasis—this is the only pond in the village—up to now birds and insects have had to make shift with such lowly beakers as waterspouts and puddles. During the summer, especially in hot weather, the Vicar's bees make their appearance, snatching an hour or two from toil to quench their thirst, for they are thirsty creatures. Sometimes the little pool by the waterfall is black with them and I do not care to venture too near. I must confess I am no bee lover and they know it. I have great respect for their sheathed and poisonous daggers, as I have for their patient industry.

From Devon and Cornwall, Scotland and Wales, I have brought green and moisture-loving plants. Pennyworts and ferns from the Devon banks, ling and thyme from Cornwall and the North. Most of them thrive, a few die.

Frogs are constant and welcome visitors to the rockery. On lifting the slab which houses the electric pump the other day I found two large toads sitting side by side on top of the engine. Apparently they liked the vibration on their tummies and maybe derived health from this free electrical treatment. Naturally the water appealed to them too and every evening a small patient figure could be seen swimming across from one side to the other, a sight which rouses my labrador Busy to a frenzy. She screws her head so far round I sometimes think it will come off. When she catches a frog on terra firma she picks it up and shakes it, though she does not harm it. Sometimes, in the summer dusk, I see her 'frogging', a pastime which seems to afford her as much pleasure as shooting. She will stand for hours by the side of the pool, or sit catlike with tail curled round, waiting for a toad to appear.

She is a lovable but foolish creature. At the periods of the full moon she seems to have attacks of madness. There is a saying in the family that Busy should be tied up at the full moon period, and there are grounds for truth in this statement. She always seems to have some laughable and clownish adventure at somebody else's expense.

The other day, whilst I was out for a walk with my wife, we met a man driving a flock of sheep. He was wheeling a bicycle and over his back he carried a sack. He had also a sheep dog with him.

Busy, as soon as she saw the sheep, ran forward to make friends with the dog. The result was as follows.

The man, losing his temper rushed at the two dogs and endeavoured to strike them with the front wheel of his bicycle. His feet slipped from under him and he fell. The bicycle flew one way, the dogs and sheep another, and he sat heavily down on the sack.

Now in the sack was a hen. Though hens may be comfortable to sit upon they appear to complain at the treatment. This hen was no exception, it complained loudly at the top of its raucous voice; so did the man, the sheep and the dogs. My wife and I retired under the confusion with a somewhat amazed Busy following after. The last thing we saw was a mud-stained and dejected figure gazing into the profound depths of the sack, whence came ever feebler complaints.

Busy at such times is capable of doing an enormous amount of damage. In a rash moment I took her to Essex where I was collecting illustration material for a book by Henry Warren, *England is a Village*.

I forgot about the state of the moon—Busy had not. In one day she upset a tea tray, broke several valuable cups, ruined our hostess's carpet, and broke one of my teeth. She finished up by being sick under the bed.

My other dog is a spaniel bitch, a curious little soul full of sighs and sorrows. I bought her from a Scotch keeper and I have reason to believe she was 'knocked about'. She is terrified of boots and sticks. Compared to Busy, she has more brains and works harder in the field, her only drawback is her mouth. Rabbiting spoilt her as it will all dogs. Once a dog catches a wounded rabbit, its mouth is ruined. But she is a lovable little creature, and though she has a somewhat hasty temper, she is always sorry afterwards.

A house without a dog is no home at all. Dogless people are usually odd. I have noticed that you can usually tell a person's character by the breed of dog they possess. There is no doubt about this, and people who like spaniels are always 'nice' people!

The joys of shooting are threefold if one has a good dog to work with and this is one of the reasons why I prefer shooting to fishing.

Of all forms of angling I like night fishing the best. It is tremendously exciting down by the dark river when the moon is just climbing over the trees. On the Border Esk I have had some enjoyable times.

At Canonbie (where incidentally there is a most comfortable hotel which caters especially for fishermen) there is excellent sea trouting, though in a bad season such as the one just passed (1940) you may come back night after night with an empty creel. I never remember the rivers so small. They had little rain during the summer and consequently the water was very low and foul. Walking up the river one day by 'Jock's Pool' I came to a rocky basin close under the bank. The water was quite shallow, only about seven inches deep and in the middle was a large stone. As I came suddenly over the bank I was amazed to see an enormous brown trout dart across, sending a furl of water before it like a miniature torpedo. It dashed under the rock. That fish must have been close on five pounds in weight.

I got a long stick and poked vigorously and eventually it streaked out across the shallows and leapt over a ledge into the peaty depths of Jock's Pool.

Two years ago I had most enjoyable sport in this place, fishing at night with a large white moth. This art of night fishing is difficult. The beginner will find that the line gets into the most hopeless tangles and it is indeed a wearisome business untangling it. After a little practice however one gets the knack. It is easy to tell after a while if your fly is going out as it should. There is a gentle pull on the line as the fly alights on the water. And if you are in luck and the trout are rising the thrill of playing a big game fish in the dark is tremendously exciting. One casts perhaps for some time before a fish takes you and then there is a sudden tug

and the shrill whizz of the reel as the line is ripped off the drum.

Out under the farther bank you feel the heavy tugging weight and now and again he will jump, showing his position by the faint gleams on the dark water.

The actual netting of the fish I find most difficult of all, because it is very hard to see the exact position of your beaten quarry. If he is spent, however, there is a dim gleam, even in the darkest night, as he lolls inert in the shingly shallows.

Fishing alone on these Border rivers is quite an eerie performance. Opposite, the dark firs rise up in an impenetrable wall, bank and foliage mingle and you cannot see the actual dividing line. Owls hoot up in the woods and some creature of the night stealthily cracks a stick.

The murmur of the waterfalls comes on the wind, now loud now faint, echoing between the rocks of the dark valley. Now and again there is a heavy splash as some huge sea trout leaps lower down the pool and the faint flicker of an electric torch far below the rapids tells of another angler in trouble with his tangled line. Or maybe you are the only rod fishing the river and there is no sign of any other human company. Over the tips of the jagged firs a faint glow appears and then the keen edge of the moon rises higher and higher. Curlew pass over on their way to the moors, their wild pipes coming down from the immensity of space.

Now that the moon has risen, the line and cast shine like gossamer and as the fly alights on the pool a faint twinkle is seen. The opposite bank is visible now, the huge tumbled blocks piled one upon another, the pale band of shingle and the splintered pine tree which lies on its side, hurled there by the force of the winter floods.

Sometimes you will hook an unheard of thing in Jock's Pool, a chub, a coarse unwieldly brute without an ounce of fight in him. They sometimes take a fly at night and I have noticed they are becoming much commoner in the Border Esk. On hot summer afternoons you may see the 'whoppers' lying on the gravelly shallows, head up stream, and at first they may be taken for big sea trout. How these fish come to be in a fast flowing river is a mystery.

Some years ago I went with two friends to Gmunden in Upper Austria. Gmunden is a most romantic town set among the pine clad mountains at the head of a large fresh-water lake. A river, the Traun, runs out of the lake over a succession of weirs crossed by wooden bridges and the continual roar of the water is one of the chief things which I remember about Gmunden.

Below the rough water, in the weir pools, were some veritable monsters. I saw one trout which my gillie told me weighed nearly twenty pounds. It was always lying in the same spot close to some piles and I have never, in all my life, seen such a fish. Curiously enough it was not of a great length but tremendously thick and deep. These fish are seldom caught on a fly and the only method is by trolling with a minnow, which is not allowed by the authorities.

We never caught any trout during the day, only a few chub and grayling. But in the evening we set forth with the gillies, picturesque folk in their short skin pants and Tyrollean hats, who carried on their backs the long wooden 'bottles' in which the trout were placed when caught. This struck me as a dreadful swindle. You were not allowed to keep your fish unless you paid for it at so much per kilo. If you caught a good one it was placed in the bottle and carried back to the fishing hut where it was duly weighed and entered in the log-book kept for the purpose. In the hut was a vast tank, full of fresh and running water, in which the trout were placed. I saw some monsters swimming round there, some weighing over eight or nine pounds. These fish were sold to the hotels in the town.

The best fishing was done from boats, flat-bottomed 'scows' which seemed very unwieldy.

At seven o'clock each evening the rise began, and the river fairly boiled with fish. One could expect good sport. The only snag was that as the water was so clear (it is a swift and deep river) one had to fish extremely fine and when you did hook a good one it broke you.

I suppose that the Traun is the finest trouting river in the world, at any rate in Europe. The average weight was round about three and four pounds and they ran very much larger, anything up to twenty pounds.

But on the whole the expedition was hardly worth the

excessive cost and the practice of appropriating one's catch most aggravating. I suppose I am too much of a 'hunter' fisherman to enjoy such sport. I like to keep what I catch and eat it too! And after all, so do most true fishermen.

But the river is beautiful and the scenery past description. Our hotel overlooked the lake, the Traunsee. After breakfast one could go out of the hotel and dive into the water, which was so clear that its depth was deceptive.

I have had some good sea-trout fishing in Wales on the Gwyfor, near Lloyd George's birthplace. I remember some good nights on this river and of my meeting with the little village schoolmaster who had caught an enormous sea-trout the night before on a lob.

'You will not catch them until the bats are out,' he told me.

When the bats are out. . . . What that saying conjures up to me! Many quiet evenings by the river in the days of peace, a June walk up the valley of the Colne near Bibury, the smell of the water meadows and trout hatcheries, when the swallows have gone to roost and even the cuckoo is silent.

Such an evening I remember, away in those times when 'blackout' and 'blitzkrieg' were unknown things.

Over Bibury mill the sun had dipped and the trout were dimpling the surface of the hatchery pools. Against the soft sky the willows were clear cut and sharp, each slender almond leaf motionless, borne on their graceful wands. The little valley was musical with the talking of the waters, in the quiet of evening their voices carried far.

A few late swallows and martins hawked above the marshy ground and everywhere the hedge parsley glimmered white in the dusk. I followed the road from Bibury to Ablington, that loveliest of all Cotswold villages. Many large bats were circling overhead, they seemed as big as swifts and flew in the same manner. I have noticed that about Bibury and the valley of the Colne the Great Bat is by no means uncommon. During the day they sleep in old barns and farm buildings and emerge in the half light. When compared with the pipistrelles they are terrifying creatures, as big as vampires.

By the time I reached Ablington it was deep dusk and the village seemed swallowed in shade from the trees. Indeed one almost had the impression that the houses had been built in the middle of a wood. Never have I seen such mountains of foliage; these Colne valley trees, mostly lime and sycamore, are splendid specimens. I do not think there is an ugly house in Ablington, at least I could not see one. Even the small cottages are beautifully proportioned, with the graded lichen-bedecked tiles which are so characteristic of the Cotswold villages.

The Colne runs under the village street, through a stone bridge. There seemed not a soul about and no lights in the village, but it was no blackout which doused the cottage lamps; the inhabitants had gone to bed. Standing by the bridge under the silent canopy of the trees the stream was loud, so loud that it drowned the approaching footsteps of an ancient man carrying a bucket. He set it down by the bridge and wished me 'good evening'. I began to ask him about the village and his life there. As a young man, he said, he had lived in Wales and worked in the coal mines. He was not a Welshman however, for he had been born in the next village to Ablington. And the love for his native country was so strong that he felt he must return to it.

So he had come back again to finish his days in this paradise. I asked him about the trout (conversation soon turns to trout in this part of the world) and without another word he took from his pocket a crust of bread, and breaking it up, threw the pieces into the stream. We watched those glimmering scraps of white borne away on the dark waters until they reached the shadows of some overhanging branches of lime trees fifteen yards distant. Then plop! plunge! one by one they vanished, sucked under by the mighty spotted beauties.

'They lie there, under those trees,' he said, 'they catch the caterpillars and things which fall off the leaves. But we can't catch them, they belong to the squire.'

We talked on until there was no light on the water and the distant chimes of a church reminded me of bed.

Bat

CHAPTER IX

Holland

Chapter IX

In the spring of 1937 a friend and I paid a visit to Holland in search of the avocet, spoonbill, and ruff.

I was disappointed in Holland. Few people who have not been there realize its dense population. For miles around the Hague the roads are lined with the neat, gaily painted Dutch houses, which are however more attractive than our bungalows.

We stayed at Den Helder, what was then the Naval Base and the equivalent of our Portsmouth, now the target for nightly attention by the R.A.F. (1941).

We liked Den Helder, though it did not of course compare with Rotterdam or Amsterdam. For the bird lover it is a good centre, for one is within reach of Friesland and Texel. We found nothing of interest in the immediate vicinity of Den Helder. But a journey by car (we shipped one with us) across the long dyke by Leuwarden to Friesland took only a few hours and there one found the unspoilt Holland, complete with windmills and long dykes, reedy meres and wide flat fields ablaze with golden dandelions.

It was not long before we saw signs of bird life. We pulled up the car on a country road to watch ruffs displaying within fifteen yards of us. The strange creatures appeared quite unbirdlike with their distended ruffs and down-pointed bills as they squatted before us on the white grit of the road.

These birds are singularly beautiful and the difference in colouration is quite unbelievable. Some were all shades of chestnut, others ebony black with snow white ruffs and vice versa, others snow white all over with perhaps a chestnut banded ruff; their variety is astonishing.

Surely of all birds the ruff is the most vain. For minutes at a time the eared and distended creatures, quite unrecognizable as birds, sit with bills touching the ground, 'hotching' round at intervals when a reeve ventures near. The drab little reeves seemed most disinterested in these antics and fed either singly or in large flocks on the adjoining meadows. We searched in vain for avocets and spoonbills; ruffs seemed the most common species, though we had interesting views of bar-tailed godwits in full golden breeding dress and a very fine 'close up' of two gargany teal swimming up a dyke.

We saw so many ruffs we became quite tired of them; it was perhaps the spoonbill we wished to see above all others. Maybe we were unlucky in our quest in Friesland, for others have told me that when they visited the same locality they saw both spoonbill and avocet in plenty. We had to go to Texel to see the avocet. On this island they breed and we had some good views of them at close quarters. They are fairylike and striking birds, graceful both in flight and on the ground.

We took bicycles with us to Texel (hired from an American garage proprietor in Den Helder) and in this way we could cover a lot of ground and miss very little of interest. We had been there a week and still we had seen no trace of the spoonbill.

And then one day, motoring near Den Helder, we saw a large white bird flying along in the distance. A glimpse through the glasses revealed the object of our journey; it was indeed a spoonbill. It alighted by the side of a dyke not far from us, and after a keen look round hopped down into it and began to wade along, scooping its spoon from side to side. It seemed extremely shy however, as wary as a wild goose, for every now and then it hopped out on to the top of the bank and eyed us suspiciously. Later we saw other spoonbills, but it seemed a rare species and I had the impression that it is dying out in Holland. As to storks we never saw one the whole time we were there.

The snag seemed to be that we could not wander about in Holland without arousing suspicion. Several times we were taken for spies and everywhere we saw Verboten notices. Most of our bird watching had to be done from the road.

Poor Holland! They had indeed cause for suspicion. Helder, Friesland, and the long dyke across the Zuider Zee, were destined to see grim happenings when the German Panzer columns invaded that contented little country, exactly three years later.

The crump of bombs and the rattle of machine guns must have disturbed the posturing ruffs along that country road by the Zuider Zee, and many a courageous Dutchman perished among the golden fields of dandelion.

Undoubtedly Texel is the best locality for birds in Holland, and there are rooms to be had on the island as we afterwards found out.

N   C.B.B.

One very interesting incident occurred whilst we were there. At one end of the island is a seaplane base (again a great target for our R.A.F. at the present time of writing) and behind it, extensive marshes, which are tidal.

One day T. K. and I were lying on the sand dunes, scanning the marshes on the lookout for uncommon birds. Avocets and godwits kept us occupied for some time and it was pleasant enough lying in the sun. Even though it was not yet mid-May the day was hot and hardly a cloud was to be seen in the sky. The smell of the marshes reminded me of my own wildfowling haunts at home and I noticed the same sea plants, lavender and samphire.

Suddenly my glasses picked out a long line of large birds far out on a sheet of tidal water near the seaplane base. This needed investigation, though I was terrified that we should be arrested, as all along the dunes were notices in unpronounceable Dutch which appeared forbidding enough.

We advanced across the marshes, stopping now and again to focus our glasses, and before very long we were having bets with each other as to what the birds were. It was certain that they were geese of some sort, but with the strong sun behind them it was most difficult to see their colour. For a long while I thought they must be grey geese and it was not until we drew within range that they all rose and flew off to the sea. They proved to be Brent geese, surely an unusual species to find in Holland in May. No doubt they were on their way North and had stopped to break their journey.

Texel was within easy reach of Den Helder by boat, though it took about three hours, as far as I remember, to get across. Wherever we went we found the Dutch a most courteous and friendly people, always ready to help in any way and most of them could speak good English.

The long dyke across the Zuider Zee became quite

familiar after a journey or two by car, for we did most of our 'birding' in Friesland. Nearly twenty miles long, it is a wonderful piece of engineering and quite the most perfect road I have driven upon. The Rover did unheard of speeds, and on the perfectly smooth surface there was no vibration.

When half-way over, one had the impression of being surrounded on all sides by open sea, and cars approaching down the dyke appeared at first as a mirage.

Only in Friesland did I see the country of Rembrandt's etchings, the same long roofed barns and farms and the village churches of almost Russian architecture. Alas! however, the old picturesque Dutch costume of velvet trousers and fur cap is no longer seen, save in the tourist centres, where the locals derive much profit from would-be 'kodakers'.

Nowhere did I get a sense of wildness and this was disappointing. I have no great wish to return to Holland.

This morning I counted no less than eleven song thrushes, three blackbirds, a cock and hen bullfinch, two species of tit (cole and great), a cock and hen chaffinch and a willow warbler all by the rockery pool. Some were bathing and others, having bathed, were sitting on the birch trees preening themselves. It was the thrushes which amused me the most. At one end of the pool, a great many leaves had fallen in and formed a solid carpet, almost a raft. The thrushes seemed to be quite mad, dashing about the margin of the pond with erect crests and fluffed out wings. To my astonishment, one settled on the leaves in the water and attempted to bathe, flirting its wings and dipping its head. It naturally sank and without more ado swam across to the other side and seemed in no way put out, for it repeated the performance a moment later and the other thrushes followed suit! Such an occurrence is difficult to explain. Usually when a bird gets its feathers very wet it is unable to fly, yet these thrushes seemed in some mysterious way to keep their wings dry.

One of them had a deformed leg, for it carried it straight out behind. Perhaps the poor creature had been caught in a trap and the thigh had been dislocated. It was interesting to see the skilful way with which it retained its balance and seemed not unduly hampered by the usless limb. One sees many birds maimed in this way. During the last winter, which was so severe on wild birds, I came across an un-speakable act of cruelty. Some people in the village keep ferrets and one day as I was passing in the snow I heard agonizing cries coming from their yard. On investigation it seemed that they had set a wire sparrow trap in the yard baited with bread and had caught one of the many starving blackbirds which hung around every door begging for food. This had been given alive to the ferrets, to make them 'keen'.

In Chapter Three I mentioned the reservoir near my home which is a favourite haunt for birds of all kinds. Above the reservoir, the infant Avon winds along through rough and marshy meadows, beloved of the peewit and the hare.

The brook is only a few feet across, but is too wide to jump and is surprisingly deep for so small a stream. Here and there are dark pools, studded in summer with yellow 'water blobs' which, when half-opened, seem like exotic poppy heads gone to seed. It is pleasant to follow the course of this brook as it winds about, full of secret recesses and hidden angles, choked in places by pallisades of green rush which quiver gently in the current. In another place, wild iris grow in dense thickets, a wonderful sight in June.

There is a favourite spot of mine where a big willow over-hangs the brook and the stream broadens out into a fair-sized pool, five feet or more in depth. Here on hot summer afternoons I have lain on the bank watching the roach and dace swimming in and out between the water lily roots and dimpling the surface after flies. At the head of the pool is a shallow which, in early summer, is alive with perch and roach fry. They are always to be found at this particular place. As the cattle come down to drink they churn up the mud, which attracts vast shoals of minute fish. One afternoon I built a low rampart of stones across the running water at a spot where it enters the main pool. I left a small opening near the bank and then churned up the mud inside my 'corral'.

In a minute or two small roach ventured near, as the clouds of mud quickly cleared, and one by one they entered the stone ring. Soon the area was alive with fry and with a quick movement I placed a net over the gap next to the bank and the little silver fish rushed headlong into it and I lifted them out on to the bank. They were mostly roach and perch as bright as freshly minted silver and perfect in every detail. Even the wee perch had the faint barring on the back. Roach and perch fry always left a pool by the way they came in, but the stickle-backs and minnows had more sense and dived through the interstices of the stone dam. But 'once caught twice shy' and after a little while not a fish would be caught again; they soon learnt by experience that it was a trap.

Some of these pools hold very big perch, fish running up to over a pound, and there is no fresh-water fish, with the exception of the trout, which has a better flavour. Perch from a pond are muddy and tasteless but these river perch are well worth catching. The flesh is a beautiful silvery white lined faintly with blue veins.

In early spring snipe come up from the big reservoirs to breed in these remote water meadows and when the eggs are incubated the male bird perches on the tops of the surrounding trees uttering a monotonous alarm note. It is indeed a queer spectacle to see the long-legged and longnosed snipe perching, like any other bird, on the top of a high tree.

Always, winter or summer, there is a heron winging his way up the river valley with the gravity and importance of a pelican. In the evening, their hoarse cries ring across the fields, where the mists begin to gather like milky blankets about the river. The nearest heronry is at Stanford Park, though I believe that now only a few birds remain.

When I first came to these parts the heronry was quite a big one but now, for some reason or another, the herons have fallen out of favour and they are not allowed to breed to the same extent, which is a great pity.

The heron is a solitary person, happy as long as he is left alone all day long to fish and sleep in the wilder river meadows. There is one field I know where the herons roost during the day. It is a remote and rushy pasture far from any road or house and here all the herons in the vicinity congregate during the afternoons to sleep and digest their meals.

This is the only time when they seem to prefer one another's company, though in the nesting season they keep together. They are known to the country people as 'storks'.

Now there is a searchlight post overlooking the river valley and whenever death comes throbbing up among the stars the unnatural 'synthetic' light pierces the darkness and casts an eerie glow on the hanging wood on the hill nearby.

The other night the Hun struck at Coventry, a raid that will surely be remembered long after this war is over. There may be other raids as bad or even more violent in the months ahead, but it was the first time the Nazi fiends gave a demonstration of their utter ruthlessness.

Soon after the November dusk had fallen we heard the throb of engines overhead and our little house trembled, as explosion after explosion racked the stricken city. Though Coventry is twenty miles away there was no thought of sleep.

Now and again a cluster of sinister and unwinking lights broke and hung in the sky beyond the doctor's house, always in the same spot between the two dark yew trees in his garden. Then the red sparks of the tracer bullets sped upwards in apparently vain endeavour to shoot them out.

Once a terrific glow shot upward and slowly sank; maybe this was the death of the lovely old cathedral. And once an enemy plane became incandescent in the sky and plunged down in flames, leaving a long thread of fire down the sky.

It was a night of clear and frosty moonlight; the Huns must have seen their prey clearly without the aid of flares. I could hear from time to time the far voice of the sergeant on the searchlight post singing out orders like a man calling in the cattle.

The throb of a raider grew nearer. Then far up among the stars a whining started which grew and grew, a tearing whine which seemed to take such a long time to reach the earth. The searchlight flicked out; at the same moment there was a roar and the house rocked on its toes. But those bombs missed the searchlight and the railway by a matter of yards, throwing masses of earth on to the line.

Every night at the same time a train comes panting down the valley. Peace or war it is always the same. And a moment after the bombs had burst I heard the old 'puffer' coming along the track.

The engine ploughed through the earth and went on its way as though nothing had happened.

This dropping of bombs in our rural countryside is wanton madness. By my old home they have dropped an 'H.E.' within three hundred yards of the house and one flying lump of lead pierced the windows, the first time the old house has ever been under fire. And that particular bomb burst right on the bank where we used to find the first violets in the spring. It was a warm field bank which faced south, where I have stalked many a rabbit with the ·22 in boyhood days. But next year there will be more wild violets blooming there to mock Hitler and his crew, and they will be blooming long after he and all his gang are turned to earth themselves.

I find comfort in these thoughts. But there, I am talking of the war. This book is to be about pleasanter things.

In every country parish there is a bank or hedge where the first violets are known to bloom. As a boy I knew not only every hedge, but every tree and bush, for some miles around my home. I know them now, though many of the trees have gone. Yet other trees have grown up; the face of the countryside is always changing.

I was very lonely as a child as my two brothers went away to school and I was left behind for reasons of health. All my free time I was out in the fields and in this way I came to know the surrounding country in an intensely intimate way.

Below the house were three large ponds, known as the 'fish ponds'. They had been there for generations and contained some hefty fish. The upper pond was choked with dense reed beds and willows, a heavenly jungle which I used to explore on frequent occasions. The pool below had an island in the middle, on which grew four, very tall, ivy-clad trees, and some dense holly bushes and a few thorns. As there was no boat we could never get to it and various attempts at boat building were nipped in the bud by the Olympians.

Wildfowl bred upon the island, safe from our reach, and

In the Woods

we knew there was an owls' nest in one of the larger trees, for we had seen the old birds flying in and out at dusk and had also heard the wheezing call note of the young owlets.

We determined to reach this island somehow or another. On the north side this seemed an impossible feat for there was a band of deep water between the reed bed close to the bank and the island itself. But on the west side there was a fallen branch which projected out across the water and almost touched the fringe of the reeds. Attempts to wade across the boggy ground met with disaster, so we built a platform of logs and sticks out from the bank. We carried tons of timber to make that platform and at last one day I managed to get my arms over the projecting branch and pull myself up upon it.

Unfortunately this branch grew downwards

Brooding Mallard

into the pool half-way over, rising again after a space to where it joined the island. It was visible however under the water, and by progressing very carefully, like a tight rope walker, it was possible to cross the submerged portion.

I got over without mishap and at last swung my legs down and found myself on the island. The whole of the earth was covered with ground ivy. I shall never forget the thrill of first setting foot on this enchanted place.

It was springtime and I knew there would be a rich reward in the shape of many nests. From under the hollybush a mallard duck scuttled and took wing and there, right under the holly, half buried in luxurious down, were six large green eggs. And we found the owls' nest, sure enough, up in a hole in the big tree, full of snapping, hissing goblins, and our first coots' nest, built on a submerged branch covered with ivy.

There were other important discoveries. An old swan's house built of wood, hidden under the holly bushes, and strangest of all, a vixen, long dead, lying at the mouth of a hole under the tree where the owl had its nest.

Two incidents stand out in my mind with regard to the 'Island'. One day, whilst poking about in the reeds, I heard the biggest croak I have ever heard in my life. It was no mere ordinary frog's croak, it sounded like a deep toned voice of a bull frog. And after a while I saw the creature, a frog of enormous size. To this day I am puzzled whenever I think of it.

We had at home in our old nursery a stuffed bull frog brought by some wandering relative who had visited America. This frog sitting in the reeds was every bit as big, indeed so vast was it that I ran all the way home in terror.

The other incident happened a few years later in the marsh above this pond. It was a curious place overgrown with giant dock, interspersed with willow thickets in which the gentle turtle dove bred every summer.

One winter's day, when frost was on the ground, I was hunting up the marsh for moorhens. I noticed a broken willow stump surrounded by dead reeds and as I paused for a moment by it I heard the sounds of eating coming from within. I peeped inside and saw a little creature about the size of a watervole. Its fur was a grey-green colour and on each side of its body were two pale stripes rather like those of a chipmunk. I tried to catch it but it ran away through the reeds and I never saw it again. What this little animal was I cannot pretend to guess for there is no member of the British rodent family which resembles it.

On another occasion, after a week of mild autumn weather, when the reed beds had been beaten down by the torrential rains and high winds, I saw a monstrous carp trapped in a shallow pool among the reeds. It was cruising round and round trying to find an exit. It was so old a fish that its scales were all 'knobbly' and it was probably as old as the pond for carp live to a great age.

We caught some good fish from these pools but no very large ones. In the lower pool there were pike, but the best we ever caught weighed only eight and a half pounds. No doubt there were other larger fish, but we never heard of them being taken.

Many wild duck bred there before the adjacent main road became so busy with traffic.

Now both ponds are nearly overgrown and the old sheep-wash at the end of the lower pool (where in the summer heats I have watched Bob Wilson, with a sack tied round his waist washing the sheep) has crumbled away. Elder bushes grow out of the ancient barrel which served as Bob Wilson's pulpit. This barrel was fastened to the wall of the sheep-wash by a massive chain and Bob, armed with a long pole pushed each sheep's head under as it reached another wooden boom which spanned the sheep-wash just at water level.

What a thrill it was to see the hapless woolly creatures herded into the pen by the stalwart yokels and led out one by one to the edge of the runway. They were hurled in from there with a mighty splash. Some tried to turn back but were poked on their way towards the man in the barrel. When they reached the boom, down came Bob's pole and under they went, their watery 'baas' and dilated eyes eloquent of the terror they experienced.

On one unforgettable day I remember a great battle on the edge of the brickwork between John Gay the shepherd and a strong and vigorous sheep. They swayed to and fro on the brink in mortal combat and I prayed that the sheep might win. My prayers came true, it did.

The sheep gave a violent plunge, with John hanging round its neck, and the next moment both fell headlong into the 'wash'. Needless to say Bob Wilson did not apply the pole and John did not have to be pushed under the boom. They pulled him out, a very draggled picture of a man and I believe he was ill afterwards in consequence.

How well I can recall that rural scene; the broad spread fingers of the horse chestnuts overhead with their erect white candles; the golden dazzle of the buttercups in the mead beyond, and the shouting of men and bleating of sheep. Sheepwash day was always hot, always at the height of summer.

Those days are gone for ever, for they do not wash the sheep now in the primitive way, and the old men have gone too, and with them the peace which once was ours.

The small fair-headed boy is a grown man and many an autumn harvest of elm and chestnut leaves lies in the bottom of the old sheepwash by the pools.

The Old Sheepwash

CHAPTER X

Faxton Church

Chapter X

From mid-November onwards, on every mild winter day,
song thrushes and mistle thrushes sing continuously. I
always find it extremely difficult to tell the difference between the song of the blackbird and that of the mistle
thrush. They are almost identical, though the mistle
thrush's notes are stronger and carry for a greater distance.

It always gives me a queer sensation to hear the spring
song of a bird in autumn or winter. Rooks are as noisy in
autumn as they are in March or April but there is a different
quality in the sound.

As a boy I collected eggs and for a long time I was unable
to obtain a rook's egg. Eggs given me were not the same,
I had to collect each specimen myself.

There were of course numerous rookeries around my
home but all were in very high trees, elms and oaks, and I
had not the 'head' or the courage to climb to them. And

then one day I came upon a rookery which was built in a spinney of ash poles far away in some wild rolling fields near a village called Faxton, mentioned later in this chapter.

These nests were built in the tops of the poles and though they were quite high enough, the task of climbing to them seemed not so difficult. The only snag was that there were no lower branches to give one a 'start' and the trees were quite smooth and extremely hard to climb. We tried swarming, but after about ten or twelve feet up, arms gave out and we came slithering down. Yet, there above us, we could see the huge bulky nests which we knew contained eggs. This spinney was about four miles from my home and could not be reached by any road, nevertheless we determined to carry a ladder all that way. It was a very long ladder and an extremely heavy one but we managed it, up hill and down valley, resting every hundred yards or so to ease our arms. After a mile or two we felt ready to drop but we carried on and at last reached the rookery. I had brought with me some six-inch wire nails and a hammer, in case the ladder proved too short.

There was fearful pleasure in this escapade because, in the first place, we had to remove the ladder from the garden without being seen, and also the owner of the spinney might at any moment make his appearance. Six-inch nails driven into ash poles destined for fencing would hardly meet with approval.

But the job was done, and at last the spinney came bobbing into view over a rise in the fields, and there we saw the circling rooks tossing against the April blue.

When we chose our 'pole', the crown of which was thick with at least ten nests, and placed the ladder against it, we found that we were still some way from the lowest branch. So standing on the top rung I drove in the nails, climbing up inch by inch, holding the green bole of the tree very

tightly with my arms. At last I reached out and caught hold
of the lowest bough and a moment later I was up among
the branches. Fifteen feet above me loomed the huge stick
structures, but as there was a considerable wind I soon began
to swing like the pendulum of a clock. A glance downwards
turned my stomach over, for I saw the white face of my
brother absurdly dwarfed, and the tiny celandines growing
on the floor of the spinney. It seemed a long way down and
I had to shut my eyes.

Cautiously I climbed higher and higher until I was just
below the nests. The branches were thin now and I half
thought they would never bear my weight. I was also terrified lest the top of the tree should suddenly swing over and
slide me off in a shower of precious eggs.

The trouble was that it was difficult to get my hand over
the edge of the nearest nest, for it projected directly over my
head like a ceiling. For some time I sat hunched miserably
in the fork trying to pluck up courage. All around, the poles
were swinging and swaying, and each time a gust came
along I shut my eyes as I swung right over. At last there
came a lull and seizing my chance I stood up in the fork and
got my hand over the edge of the nest. Oh joy! EGGS! A
whole clutch of warm smooth eggs! Surely it must have
been a boy who first coined the term 'clutch'!

I have read that the climbers on Mount Everest experienced no great elation when they were within reach of the
summit, their reactions were dulled and listless. At that
moment I felt very much the same. My one desire was to
get down to the friendly ground and have done with this
nightmare. I am afraid I rifled the nest, hardly daring to
look at my hard-won prize before I thrust them into my
egg box.

From far below however came a voice urging me to in-
vestigate the other nests. Whilst I was up there, think of the

opportunity! And I did manage to get to two other nests, all of which contained eggs.

Soon the giddiness began to leave me and I could look around. To be up on the level of a rookery was a most thrilling experience. On all sides I could see nests, some on a slightly lower level so that I could see the eggs. And all about me was the clashing of the poles in the wind and the

Rookery

cawing of rooks as they swung overhead with outstretched wings.

Then I slithered down, and what joy it was to feel the soft boggy ground underfoot and brush the green dust from my clothes! And greatest joy of all was when I laid out my spoils on the celandines, and pored over the infinite variety of green-blotched eggs laid all a-row!

We made the journey back in record time and got in without being seen or caught by the Olympians. The eggs were blown with a blow pipe and drill and they still grace my cabinet, a perpetual proof of skill and daring! To a boy, such happenings are of tremendous import, and remain in the memory until old age.

Looking back however I realize now how unobservant are most boys. It was not until a very long time afterwards that I came to recognise the various species. I longed for a white-throat's egg but could never find the nest. And then, when I became more observant and took the trouble to lie in wait and watch, I found all the nests I wanted. It is really the laziness of the immature child mind which fails to notice things intelligently.

Egg collecting seems to be losing favour with the present generation; boys are not so keen on natural history as they used to be. Bird watching seems to have taken the place of egg collecting, but no boy gets the same thrill out of it, and a 'spitfire' is more exciting than a bird or beast.

There is a great sense of satisfaction in lying in wait for a bird, watching it on to the nest and then collecting a much desired egg yourself. Little harm is done if only one is taken from the clutch, and I know I spent many joyful hours in going over each specimen in my cabinet and recalling the circumstances of its acquisition. The sparrow-hawk's egg which I got from Cowper's spinney under the very nose of the keeper; the great crested grebe's egg from the big reservoir, which I took whilst being pursued by the water bailiff; all those eggs meant much to me.

It was a long time before I was allowed a gun and my first was a crazy ·22 of Belgian manufacture. This rifle eventually blew up and injured my eye.

Then came a ·410 cum ·22, an atrocious gun which must have cost less than twenty shillings new. It was given to me by the gardener and with it I did amazing slaughter.

Rabbits and moorhens were my chief quarry. I stalked the former on the summer evenings when they were out at feed, and those stalks were skilfully carried out, because I had to get within ten yards of the rabbit if I was to make sure of a kill. It is no easy thing to crawl up to a rabbit when the only cover is a clump of nettles or a tuft of grass. But I managed it on many occasions, and learnt how to make use of 'dead' ground.

As to moorhens, I knew all their little tricks of diving and coming up under a fallen branch or weed, or creeping away under cover of the bushes.

I have a theory that in recent years the moorhen is alter-ing its habits. It seems to prefer to roost in trees, and often when I have been pigeon shooting in the woods I have seen a moorhen walking about in the upper branches.

Where foxes abound, the moorhen nearly always roosts up in bushes and trees and sometimes will build their nests in willow bushes for the same reason. Though it is not a sporting bird because its flight is slow and ungainly, yet they are excellent eating and are quite as 'gamey' as pheasant if hung long enough. For my part I prefer them to snipe or woodcock. An old saying, frequently re-quoted, has it that the moorhen can foretell floods and so builds its nest high in the willows. The real reason is to keep their eggs and young out of the reach of foxes and rats.

Then came the days of pocket money, half a crown a week, which was rigorously put by until I had collected nearly enough to buy a twelve bore. I still needed about thirty shillings however and the problem was how to raise the necessary cash.

Visiting uncles unwittingly gave rise to hammering hearts and dry mouths, especially when they took their de-parture without the looked for 'tip'.

I went through my book-case and staggered into the neighbouring market town with sundry B.O.P.'s, 'Captains' and natural history works, and by this means I at last accumulated the desired sum. What a day that was when I sent off the envelope and the money (in notes) to a firm in Birmingham! There followed agonizing days of waiting. I had not told a soul of what I had done and when, after a week, no gun arrived, I felt black despair. I must have shown it in my face, for there were questions as to whether I 'felt well'. After ten days had passed I began to realize my money had either been stolen or gone astray. Two years of self denial, scraping and saving had been in vain.

The battered little cash box was empty, I was faced with complete disaster. When I had almost given up hope I saw, one day, the postman coming down the drive with a long parcel. I rushed out and saw it was addressed to me. The gun had arrived. Trembling fingers undid the knot (I had carried my precious heavy burden into the shrubberies) and in a moment or two I saw my gun lying among the shavings; a brand new gun, heavy, blued and lethal, fragrant with 'three in one' oil.

There was to be no more crawling behind nettles to within ten yards of my prey. That evening I shot a rabbit with my first shot out of the gun, at a range of thirty-five yards. When it rolled over and I staggered across to pick it up, my ears still ringing with the report and blood filling my mouth (I had not held the gun tight enough into my shoulder), I experienced a true sense of triumph which is still with me. There is no other joy to compare with the 'first gun'.

One day in the Easter holidays my twin brother reported that he had seen a strange bird building a nest on the island of the lower fishpond. It was small and round with a yellow spot on its bill, a species we had not seen before.

This island was considerably smaller than that on the middle pool and was quite inaccessible without a boat, even our bridging operations could never reach it, for there was a wide stretch of deep water on all sides and no fallen branch which would act as a pontoon.

Growing on the bank were several tall willows and when I climbed one of these I could see the nest, built among some partly submerged yew branches, close to the island. Through glasses I could see it contained two eggs. What the bird was I could not guess, but from its reddish head I thought it must be a pochard. Pochards however do not build their nests on sunken branches and we could not identify the bird. The main question was how to reach the nest, for reach it we must. We put our heads together and determined to build a boat. We 'scrounged' all the petrol cans we could lay our hands upon and lashed these to planks of wood, binding the whole affair with stout cord. I was chosen to essay the passage as nobody else dared go. The raft was launched and found to float and very soon I was aboard, paddling with an improvised oar. The craft proved extremely efficient, for my elder brother had worked out, by mathematics, how many empty petrol tins would be required to float the weight of a man.

There was a strong wind blowing and quite a choppy sea broke inboard, but I paddled across and soon reached the island. I drifted alongside the nest and took an egg. It was no pochard but a little grebe. No doubt we should have had many other trips on board the raft, but those in authority got wind of it and it was dismantled.

There was another pool not far away, a square pond, next to a wood. We never dreamt that it contained fish until one day I saw a big pike jump close inshore and roach scattered in all directions. We went down with tackle and soon caught several large pike, as many as we could carry away. The pond had not been fished for years and they were quite uneducated.

We had a gardener then called Perkins, a great pal of ours and a keen pike fisherman. One autumn evening he had a good 'run' in this pool and the pike took his rod right out into the middle. We could not reach it, but next morning we found the rod had drifted close in to the reeds. We got hold of it and pulled in the line and found the pike was still on the end and it was landed successfully.

Perkins had an ancient single barrel muzzle loader which he kept locked up in a cupboard under the stairs of his toolshed. In the early mornings he used to shoot the woodpigeons as they came into the big cedar on the lawn in front of the house. He made all his own fishing tackle, including the reel, which ran on bicycle ball bearings. For a rod he used a gigantic bamboo and for line, packing thread. With this paraphernalia he used to catch some good pike and perch. The only snag was, that every time he threw out his pike bait, the reel overran and he spent the next half hour untangling it, with many oaths, from behind the drum.

His method of striking a fish was just as primitive. He used to say that you must 'whip' a pike and 'whip him 'ard'. As soon as the floats dived away he would grip the rod and wait for a moment or two to let the fish get well hold. Then with a mighty jerk he swung his rod point back with such force that I have sometimes seen him pull a big pike clean out of the water, as though it were a perch.

Sometimes even the pack thread would not stand the strain and the pike would depart with all his tackle.

One place above all others which affected me very strongly as a child was a village called Faxton. This village (if village it could be called) was set right away in the lonely rolling fields. No road led thither save a rutted cart track and even this petered out after a short distance.

My father used to drive over every Sunday afternoon to

take a service in the ancient church and very often I went with him. A local farmer-cum-wheelwright drove us in his trap, one, Will Hedge.

Will was a great favourite with us, he loved boys as he had none of his own, only a large family of girls.

He had fought in the Boer War and on the outbreak of the Great War he joined up again. We used to write to each other and I have a photograph by me now of Will, on horseback, taken in Flanders in the winter of 1917. He came through without mishap, but the life in the trenches undermined his health and paved the way for Bright's disease, of which deadly complaint he died a few years after the armistice.

It was a long drive to Faxton, first down a country lane under the big oak tree—which still stands—then past gorse bushes, full of linnets, to the beginning of the fields. These fields are more in the nature of a wold (indeed a neighbouring village bears the name of Wold) and are 'billowed' like the waves of the ocean. This was a relic of the Napoleonic wars, when the fields were ploughed up and drained for the growing of corn. The 'buggy' used to take these furrows like a ship at sea.

Lonely and wild, these uplands were particularly fascinating, for they were unlike anything else we had nearer home, they seemed to belong to a foreign country. Parched and bone-dry in the hot summers, dotted for miles by large ant hills, they put me in mind of some veldt or African plain. Perhaps this was because Will used to tell us, as we dipped up and down over the hillocks, of his Boer War days, of the tall ant hills on the veldt and his skirmishes and high adventures under the burning rays of the African sun.

There was little bird life on these uplands save peewits. During the early part of the summer the adult birds wheeled and tumbled about us, uttering their wild and anxious cries, for they had young among the bare ant mounds.

These strange plumed birds seemed so in keeping with the foreign aspect of the place. No matter how hard we searched we could never find their nests. When my father went into the church to take the service we were free to wander round the fields and year after year we searched for the plovers' nests but never found them. And then, one afternoon, as we drove across the furrows, I saw a young plover, unable to fly, running behind an ant hill. I jumped from the buggy and caught it, a beautiful little creature striped like a tabby.

The strange church was visible from a mile or more distant, a church without a tower but with a belfry at one end with two arches. In each arch hung a bell, one of which was dumb. Behind the church grew some tall elms, astonishingly brave trees and very lofty. High up on top of this plateau they had ridden out many a wild winter gale, their crowns black with rooks' nests. These ancient trees were full of holes in which innumerable jackdaws build; the sexton's wife had a tame one which we always visited every time we went to the church. It had fallen out of the nest and she had taken it in and reared it. About a hundred yards from the church, on the eastern side of a meadow, were the old alms houses, windowless and roofless, the home of a pair of white owls.

As far as I remember there were only about four cottages in the village and these were some way from the actual church, right out in the green fields. As we neared the village the single bell began to toll and the inhabitants could be seen coming across the level meadow, all dressed in their Sunday best, each with a prayer book, well scrubbed and arrayed in their Sabbath minds. Latterly there was nobody to toll the bell, and my father had to ring it himself. He would dismount from the buggy and enter the church, the congregation standing on each side of the little wooden gate and following in behind. I used to watch the old black bell suspended in its stone belfry with an awful fascination.

When it began to swing, the sound of its melancholy cracked note floated out far and wide across the Sunday wold.

To the unimaginative adult the tolling of the bell would have meant nothing and conjured up no mental images. But to me each stroke brought forth a mental picture and coloured the passing seconds. All the queer history of the village, its very soul, was in that melancholy sound, in it was a wild sadness and all the weariness of time, and the changing pattern of the years and seasons, the mysteries of life and of death. It filled me with a vivid uneasiness, almost a fear, and as the wind softened or loudened it, so its poignancy was the more impressive. Even now I cannot listen to distant bells without a recurrence of this feeling, for in the voices of bells there speaks a nameless ineffable sadness akin to the piping of the wind; no other man-made sound has this 'natural' quality and sense of antiquity.

And as at a given signal, the cattle feeding in the fields would, with one accord, come trooping one by one to gather along the low church-yard wall, blowing, mooing, and gingerly sniffing the nettles which grew in the ditch. I think the cows enjoyed Sunday as much as the villagers, for it was the one day in the week when there was any excitement.

Not far from the church were some low green mounds, all that remained of the once great manor house which stood at that spot. Thorn trees grew on the banks and a few more elms, not such old trees as those which grew by the church, but the rooks built there too and no doubt they were the outposts from the main rookery.

How the sun beat down on the springy grass! No shade anywhere save from the old thorn trees on the bank. Few birds were ever seen, save greenfinches, which for some reason or another always seemed to be singing by the double mounds. What was the story of this forsaken place; why had the manor house crumbled beneath the turf and the alms houses fallen down?

When the Black Plague smote London in 1665 a family fled from the stricken city and came to Faxton. They must have had some connection with the place, they must have known it. Away in those evil sinister streets, where the rattle of the gruesome carts on the cobblestones and the mournful cries of 'bring out your dead' seemed like the dreadful trappings and furnishings of a foul dream, the thought of the village, set away on its breezy uplands, must have given hope and a chance of life. So they fled away and came to Faxton, which was then a place of considerable size (indeed some say it was a town) and, with what must have been a sigh of relief, they settled down and tried to forget.

What a change it must have been to come to this haven set in the wide rolling common-land, to feel the clean breezes sweeping over the grass and hear the rooks calling their autumn caws in the elm trees!

But the dark spectre had followed them unseen, had stalked beside them over the shining sward. Soon the doom of Faxton was sealed. Whole families were wiped out and the terror-stricken survivors fled away to find some other place.

The dark spectre plied his scythe and laid the community low and did not steal away until his foul work was done. Like a stoat he had followed his prey, and like a stoat he departed, leaving Faxton a deserted and forgotten place. And so it remains today.

This sinister story made a deep impression on my mind

and often, when playing about in the sunshine among the hot grass, I used to feel the place might still be unclean.

In the church, which was a barn-like edifice with tall lancet windows filled with plain glass (criss-crossed with leads), was a memorial tablet to the Lord of the Manor, who lived in the great house nearby. Round the kneeling alabaster figures the walls had been painted black and I used to think that this was a reminder of the dread disease which had destroyed so many innocent country people.

The Lord of the Manor was one Judge Nicholls who met his end under rather mysterious circumstances whilst on circuit in Cumberland. Contemporary writers say that he was found drowned and hint at murder and acts of vengeance.

Here again there was the sinister quality which seemed to surround everything to do with Faxton. I dimly felt the presence of the Judge, who must have walked where I was walking and who lived and breathed and was aware, even as I was, of the sunlight, rooks, and glittering trees. Imagination rode away with me, to the last dread chapter of his life and his awful end. Perhaps in his dying seconds he thought of Faxton set in its breezes and rippling grass. And now I was here, in the same spot, 300 years later, gazing up at the alabaster figures in the dim interior of the church, one half of me longing to be outside, in the sun and the sweet wind.

Sometimes during the service, bats fluttered round the high altar; they lived in the wooden rafters of the roof.

On one side of the nave was an enormous iron stove with a crooked pipe which went out through a mullioned window. In winter it smoked abominably and sometimes the service had to be suspended or postponed because of the evil acrid fumes which it emitted. It often happened that a cow came in to join the service and had to be ejected by the sexton; once a great branch, from the elm outside, crashed through the roof.

In the sexton's little cottage behind the church I first heard the wireless. They had a crystal set, the first I believe in the parish, and putting on the ear phones I heard a jazz band playing.

'That's Paris that is,' said the sexton proudly, 'wonderful ain't it?'

I sat speechless, overcome with the ingenuity of mankind. To think that in Faxton, of all places, I should first hear the wireless, an invention which was to revolutionize the whole of man's outlook and thought!

Driving back across the billowing fields with Will I could talk of nothing else, and for weeks afterwards I told my friends how I had heard that band, playing in Paris.

I always felt that Faxton should be haunted, indeed I am sure it was. The sunlight had never the same friendly quality there, the birds, trees, and meadow grasses were alien and unfriendly.

There was a small horsepond not far from the church where I used to hunt for tadpoles. It was a very ordinary pond, but, to a boy, a magical place. Some squalid human tragedy took place at this spot, a baby's body was found drowned.

When I heard this story I shunned the pond, in fact I became terrified of it, and the sinister influence of Faxton was increased twofold.

One foggy afternoon my father was driving back from taking the service. Faxton in sunlight and hot summer weather was bearable, on a November afternoon the fields were thick with ghosts. As he passed the pond something caught his eye.

A tiny white figure, with arms imploringly outstretched, rose from the surface of the water, hung a moment, then slowly sank from sight. Other men might have whipped up the horse and galloped on. Not so my father. He pulled up and dismounted from the buggy, his eyes on the pond. At last he had seen a ghost, he had always wanted this to happen. As he watched, standing alone in the dripping dusk, the figure rose again, the arms still outstretched. He advanced towards it but it sank again from sight. And then he saw what the apparition really was.

Standing in the water facing him was an old cow with a white face. Every time it raised its head the drowned baby appeared.

So it was no ghost after all.

The Faxton fields held hares, an animal we never found nearer home, and we usually put one up below the church.

It was essentially right I should see my first wheatear on the wold, a true bird of the desert, reminiscent of Egypt and sunbaked lands. It flew from ant hill to ant hill, its rump as white as a bullfinch, the breast the colour of reflected sunlight.

About two miles from Faxton, to the north of it, was a very ancient farm with a large tower known as the hawking tower. Tradition had it that in the old days the nobles used to fly their hawks from the top of it, the game being put up by beaters. One day I climbed to the roof and got out on to the leads. Here I made a great discovery. Marked in the leads at various places were the footprints of square-toed Jacobean shoes. These footmarks must have been made when the lead was hardly set, though why or how they came to be there, no man knew. The hawking tower had always been a romantic place, now it was doubly so.

Close to the tower was a thick wood where the first primroses bloomed, a favourite roosting place for the winter pigeon flocks.

Every day the village postman tramped to Faxton. He

Hunting Hedgehog

P   C.B.B.

was a wonderful man, for though his rounds were so extensive he scorned a bicycle and preferred to go on foot. November fog or July heat Bob never missed his round and though he knew the path across the wold like the palm of his hand there were times when he lost himself. In the quick dusk of winter, when the fog lay on those bleak uplands in an impenetrable cloak, it was hard to keep direction. Once he was lost all night, wandering about from field to field and hedge to hedge, and at dawn found himself at a remote farmhouse miles away from his usual beat.

I believe that now the motor van drives to Faxton, though how it manages to cross the boggy gateways in the winter I do not know. My father has lost many pairs of goloshes in the Faxton mud and many a back axle has been broken on the rolling 'billows' over which Will used to sail in his buggy with such swooping ease.

And talking of Faxton mud brings me to a very human tale which concerns a labouring man who lived in the village some time ago.

I am indebted to my father for this story and it was broadcast by him over the wireless. I will give it in his own words. . . .

'He was a ruddy lump of a chap was Rube, but his old granny, with whom he shared one of the four dilapidated cottages which droop around the deserted village green, said: 'He were a good lad as niver give no one no trouble.'

It was difficult to find out what he thought, or if he thought, for his vocabulary was scanty, and he always preferred a grin or a grunt to a word. Owing to his outward earthiness, and his preference for hedgerows, one generally came on him unexpectedly.

When the wind shivered through the frozen bents, one might track his juicy footsteps across Daverel's Close, or Tinker's Acre, or maybe meet him, bowed under a monstrous bush of faggots, dragging his clotted feet out of the mire, an uncouth caryatid, darkling against the bilious sunset.

On Sunday, unearthed and polished, armoured in black cloth and redolent of moth ball and yellow soap, he pulled the church bell as soon as the parson's hat rose over the edge of the wold, and the grazing beasts gathered along the graveyard wall and speculated on the weekly mystery.

The iron-mouthed old woman, his granny, ordered his goings and kept a tight hand on his slender wage, ruling him with few words. For his sake she kept erect on her feet long after they should have been at rest in a hospital cot, but though hard, she was not imperishable.

One night as he lumbered homewards across the mounds on the green, when the little brown chrysanthemums were smelling strongly in the dusk, a waiting woman called to him over her garden gate.

'If I was you, Rube, I sh'd goo fer a doctor. Yer Gran's very middlin'.'

He found her huddled across her chair by the empty grate. Her eyes were closed, below the black chenille net lying awry on her bowed white head. Her hand, yellow and wrinkled as a fowl's claw, fretted at her red-checked apron.

'I sh'd goo fer a doctor, gran,' he said.

'Feed them fowls fust,' was her only feeble comment. So the hungry tired lad slid his basket down on the red quarries, and squelched off across the great fields, over Loampits, Darnal, and the Long Headland, on his four mile tramp to the surgery.

When he got back, all was black and still in the cottage. Groping his way to the mantelshelf for matches, his hand touched something cold, very cold. With a creeping at his spine he turned back through the grey door opening, and stood moveless under the dim stars, watching for the lights of the doctor's car. It was a long half hour before they glimmered in the distance and it seemed almost as long again before the glint of a flashlight down by the brook signalled the advent of a very muddy and testy man.

'You've fetched the wrong man, my lad,' he said.

'What you want is an undertaker, not a doctor. Here, some of you women, this is your job.'

A white apron flitted in from the dark like a grey owl. 'Best goo up the green a bit, Rube,' said someone, strangely gently. So Rube plodded heavily up to the top cottage, and the woodman, who had fought him at Michaelmas, shared his supper beer with him.

When the inquest was over, and Granny had been tucked up in her last bed among the nettles, the dazed lad, suffering from crowds, and from too much (and too mixed) sympathy, passed the night under the haystack on Fancy Darnel.

When the sun awakened him he went back to the cottage, and carried his granny's armchair up to the woodman (just to prevent him seeing things that weren't there), even before he cut his breakfast from the flitch in the chimney corner or emptied out four pounds twelve and fivepence from the abdominal cavity of the china dog.

The instinct of normality and force of habit kept him at his familiar work for the next three days, but the internal pressure was rising, and on the Saturday afternoon he walked to the nearest post office with an air of subdued bravado and sent away postal orders, totalling eighteen shillings and sixpence to Glasgow for a thing called a 'melodeon'.

Then ensued a period of naked, uncomfortable liberty, a dream state, in which one walked across the kitchen—aye and upstairs too—without taking off one's boots; one had meals when one wanted them; one emptied the whole pickle bottle unchidden; one spat where one chose; one smoked in bed; and one doused the brief candle by throwing one's boots at it.

At sundown on Monday the rain started. By Wednesday the kitchen and the garden had made up their long estrangement and the garden was getting upstairs by dollops. Things got a bit crowded. There was scarcely room on the table for the earthy loaf, and the paraffin had sneaked into the margarine. On Thursday night Rube was really compelled to leave his boots downstairs, and on the same night he burnt the back out of a good waistcoat, by throwing it at the candle. There was not a dry hour between Thursday night and Saturday noon. Then there was the church to sweep, the stove to lay and light, and the bell to pull, a thing which demanded drastic personal renovation. The crisis came when the clock which he had wound every night for the past ten years by pulling its rattling chain, 'ca'd canny' in the middle of striking seven. The lad had just returned from a fruitless journey to the Post Office, where there was a great silence from Glasgow; he had forgotten to take in any bread, he could not find the tin opener, and the reek of wet wood stung his throat and eyes. Now the clock had gone over to the enemy.

He looked at the thing as if it had uttered an insult. His eye fell on his axe, and in a few moments he had abolished the clock, works, case and all. His final swipe at the pedestal produced a clash of coins and there splashed about the kitchen tiles forty-two pounds ten shillings in gold, and six pounds eight in silver, from the ruins of an old oaken saltbox housed in the bottom of the case.

By the time Ruben had laboriously arrived at this total, the clock would (or should) have been striking ten, if he had not previously done the striking. But his outburst seemed to have aroused some latent Viking strain within him, for when he had knotted his wealth in a red handkerchief he commenced to tear down the contents of the cottage and to cast them into the corners of the kitchen. There was method in his madness, for now and again he looked fixedly at what he was handling before he sent it flying to the chimney corner, or behind the door. When he ceased work he had made three heaps.

Included in the first were the objects of the hate of a lifetime; the china dog (an ungrateful touch), an oleograph of Little Samuel, two purple glass vases, some framed funeral cards and the greater part of a looking glass.

The second, the largest pile, comprised the things he neither hated or disliked. There were his tools, smoothed and wasted by wear, his polished axe and billhook, his bright spade, a few black copper pots, a wooden costrel, his long leathern leggings and a round-topped lanthorn.

The third corner held the smallest pile, for there he put the things he liked and the poor have few treasures. At the bottom was his feather bed, and on it was the cage containing the cock linnet. The bird gaped silent imprecations at him, after the manner of these little creatures when one awakens them in the dark, but resigned itself again to slumber when Ruben's Sunday clothes fell over it.

The heaps having been surveyed, and some transfers made by way of adjustment, the axe was once more brought into play and all the hated objects were 'strafed'. Then the bed, the birdcage, and as many more valuables as possible, were tied on and about the bicycle. For the last time he faced his ancient enemy as, with set teeth, he stumbled out into the rain. Down the slimy foredrift into the plashy grass he struggled, the wind pushing his unwieldly burden, the terrified linnet clinging desperately to its rocking foothold. The rank drenched tussocks impeded every step.

Down by the dingle the flooded stream nearly had him over, racing past his knees, but hate carried him through.

Up the slippery avenue; dark as the nether pit, stopping every few steps to clear the clots of mud from the forks of his cycle, and along the ruts of the lane he shoved the bulging heap like an entombed insect struggling to the surface.

The clock of the neighbouring village had struck midnight when Will, the farmer-wheelwright, heard a voice calling his name above the hiss of the rain on the thatch.

'Who's there?' said he, opening the casement.

'It's me, Rube . . . I'm agoin' to Lunnon.''

'O ye are are ye? Well, do you know wot's the fust thing as'll 'appen to you in Lunnon?'

'No . . . dunno as I do . . . wot'll 'appen?'

'The police will arrest ye under the Street Noises Act for a-wearin of them boots.'

'O . . . . 'Adnt thought o' that, Will. They're new uns, that's why. But I'm got the old uns here and I'll change 'em. I'll leave the new uns fer you. They're good uns, Will. An' you can have all as I've left in the cottage. Goo you and get 'em afore they know.'

It is something over seventy miles to London, but Rube, toiling between the bed and the birdcage, arrived there the following afternoon. The bed served him to die upon two years later when bad air and unaccustomed drink had sapped his splendid health.

But the cock linnet, a staunch teetotaller, still lives.

So ends the story of Rube, surely a classic of its kind in the simple annals of the poor.

Not very far from Faxton was a large and rambling wood, a queer sort of place, swampy underfoot and with strange deformed trees which had never reached any great height. The underwood was of dense blackthorn, so impenetrable that it was quite impossible to make any headway through it, save on hands and knees. No wood is so thick that you cannot progress in this fashion, and it used to be a habit of mine as a boy—and sometimes even now—to crawl along the paths into the very heart of the thickest wilderness.

These woodland runways were mostly moss-grown, but full of sharp thorns which dropped from the overarching bushes. Each foot of the way had to be examined by touch before putting down the hand or knee.

It was not surprising that I found so many things of interest in these animal-like wanderings. I was like a woodland animal myself, save that I had not their wonderful sense of smell. Nests were easily seen from below; the frail fibre hammock of the bullfinch; the flimsy platform of turtle dove and wood-pigeon; the deep grass cup of blackcap and whitethroat, all were seen and noted.

Standing on the outside of the bushes these nests would have been quite invisible. It was amusing to see just above one's head, the grey body and black-tipped wedge tail of a portly wood-pigeon, and when she flew off with a tremendous bustle of wings, the pinkish eggs could be seen shining through the twigs. It often happened that the brooding cushat would see me below and twist her head, reminding me of a blue-grey jug, staring down at me with honey-gold eyes full of the most abject fear.

The little birds of the thorny wilderness would sometimes allow me to catch them on the nest. One little bird which was by no means uncommon was the lesser whitethroat. Their eggs are not unlike those of the garden warbler, beautifully marbled with lavender grey and greenish blotches, mostly arranged in a zone round the cap of the egg. I could creep upon the hen nightingale, sitting her olive clutch, and mark the robin-like head with the round dark eye, staring at me from among the ground ivy. Sometimes a jay would mark my passage, though I moved as stealthily as a wood mouse, and he would shriek and tear the green silences with his hideous sneaking racket.

I have met hedgehogs down these secret green runways, and bumble bees, frogs and stoats, and often have I surprised the woodland rabbits face to face.

The wood held a great mystery, indeed, an enchanting mystery. Somewhere in the very heart of this thorny wilderness there was—so the old people said—a ruined church and churchyard. They said (the ancient woodcutters and the like) that the arched doorway still stood, and the grave-stones were still visible.

No small wonder I crept so fearfully down my secret paths, peering this way and that in the green twilight! Outside the sun might still be shining but it was dark down below, as though I were under a green ocean. I stopped at times to listen, imagining that I heard the tolling of a ghostly bell, for some said the bell could still be heard in the quiet of the summer nights, pulled by ghostly hands.

I think this was the only wood in which I felt afraid and sometimes I have panicked and rushed out into the sunlight and vibrant fields, among the dancing meadow browns, where the yaffle laughed in the bright noonday.

I have searched in bare winter time for that forsaken church and I wish, I only wish, I could tell here of how I at last found it. Alas! I never did.

Perhaps it was an old wives' tale and there was no church, but I know that I never properly explored some parts of the wood; it was impossible to keep a sense of direction. Even in winter, it was too thick to walk through, and I could not follow the now muddy woodland paths. It was only when the ground was dry and the moss soft and green, that I could follow, animal-like, the winding rabbit runs.

A field or two away from this magic spot there used to be a road which once connected the hamlet of Faxton to another village, on the Duke of Buccleuch's property. The road had long vanished under the turf, though here and there its presence was betrayed by a slight hollow in the sward. The trees that lined it on either side were planted by one of the old Dukes, who earned the name of Planter John. Many of these trees still stand, and in one place they march across the fields in a grand avenue. This again was an unusual and fascinating haunt of mine; the noble trees, well proportioned and spaced out with dignity, attracted me.

Always, even on the hottest summer day, there was a breeze blowing there, and many an afternoon have I lain in the cool shade dreaming away the golden hours.

Painted Ladies seemed to love this cool avenue of oaks. They careered over the grass at an amazing pace, so quickly that the eye could scarcely follow them. Why did they resort to the avenue? There were no flowers there that I could see to attract them, no thistles or scabious, simply rippling grass where the sheep browsed, or the big white and brown cattle grouped beneath the trees lazily chewing the cud with half-closed eyes. We called it the Place of Peace.

It was indeed a place of peace, summer peace and sweet content. Trees, as I have said so many times over, lend enchantment. Remove this avenue and the open fields would have been commonplace and ordinary, like all the other bare-faced pasture land about this high ground.

Thrice blessed old Planter John. He must have known that he would never enjoy this avenue, that others would reap the benefit of his industry and careful planning. There are few of his kind today. Those old nobles must have loved the soil and the green earth to plant and plant for their descendants. Perhaps one day this true love for the earth will return. As for old Planter John, I feel his calm spirit must still walk, at times, in the Place of Peace.

When the sun throws long shadows right across the mead and not a leaf is stirring perhaps he paces, shadowless, down the long avenue, and only the feeding rabbits raise their heads, interested but without fear.

Snail Shells

CHAPTER XI

The Skeins coming in to Feed

Chapter XI

I have just been looking through my shooting journal and
give here the account of a moonlight night on the river.

The month is January, 1939, and I quote it because it
made a very deep impression on me at the time.

After being out all day with Charles, chasing greylags on
the fields, we decided to try the long breakwater for geese
under the moon. It was one of the most perfect nights I
ever remember, with the moon at the full, riding a clear
sky. We left the car outside the farm, rugged it up well with
three rugs, and set off down the lane past the big barns. It
was freezing hard and the usually muddy lane was bound
iron-hard, the moon shining on the ice. We had had a good
meal and were fit enough for anything; I somehow felt we
should see some sport of some kind, for by the sounds from
the river a great many geese were 'in'.

Our way led past the workmen's cottages, which glowed a
friendly orange from their windows, and then along the top
of the sea bank. Trees were on all sides; oaks, beech, and
birch, and their shadows laced the path before us in stripes
and bars of black.

Now and again one had a glimpse of the wide reed beds and the river, shining bright in the moonlight, and some mallard were visible as they rose from a little spring at the foot of the bank. All the way along the narrow path the grass was crisp and white. I had a great sense of well-being and excitement; the frosty night, the dark interlacing shadows, the sense of freedom and the prospect of sport went to my head. If we wished, we could stay out all night, if night it could be called, for it seemed as bright as day.

The murmuring of innumerable fowl came over the river, croakings of geese, quackings of mallard and occasionally the tearing 'scaape scaape' of a rising snipe. Sometimes too, when one stood still and listened, the whistle of passing wings could be heard; these would be duck going out to the hill bogs and burns.

Against the luminous sky the tracery of the trees was clearly visible, every twig and branch was clear-cut, laced with brilliant stars. One's breath was a white smoke in the moonlight, and the barrel of the gun searing cold. There was a considerable amount of underwood growing on the bank below, dark masses of holly and box which must have afforded snug cover for many sleeping birds. Sometimes, if the tree tops were searched with the eye, the dark form of a roosting pigeon could be seen, puffed out into a ball. It was a considerable walk to the breakwater, the path went on and on, twisting this way and that between the trees.

Where the beeches grew there was a dark mass in the hedge. This was a hide, built no doubt by my old friend Bob Kennedy, who had permission to shoot the pigeons here. I believe he got large numbers in the autumn and must have made quite a bit, for he took them into a poulterer's in the neighbouring town.

The moonlight was so clear I could peep inside the dark doorway and see empty cartridge cases lying on the floor among the straw, and a bunch of grey pigeon feathers. The path now took a bend to the right, down a slight dip where a little stream was babbling in the frosty quiet, then up again left-handed. I knew we were getting near the breakwater, another two hundred yards and we would be there.

Though the night was so cold we were both sweating in our thick clothes. We were warm enough now but later, after lying out on the cold stones, we should be frozen.

The best clothing for wildfowling has yet to be devised. I believe the Americans have invented the ideal shooting suit, which consists of a loose fitting, thick felted blouse known as a windbreaker, a peaked cap with ears, not unlike a ski-ing cap, thick breeches and high laced leather boots. If one is too warmly clad, with thick overcoats and pullovers, it is extremely hard to shoot, indeed it is almost impossible to lift the gun to the shoulder.

I favour a khaki balaclava helmet made of wool, a thick leather waistcoat and a khaki coat, and long thigh boots of rubber in which I put newspaper. This latter tip is well worth remembering. Unless one has newspapers to absorb the perspiration the waders will become wringing wet in a very short time and will cause the most agonizing rheumatism. A 'wodge' of paper, roughly cut to the size of the foot, will not only absorb all excess moisture but it will also keep the feet wonderfully warm. I also wear a thickness of paper wrapped round my body under my pullover. All this may sound rather unnecessary, but only those who have spent a night out on the marshes in frosty weather have experienced the dreadful marrow-freezing cold.

A thing one must be careful about is getting very hot through walking. One perspires freely and then, on sitting out in the reeds during a hard frost, the sweat freezes in the pores with dire results. I remember getting a touch of pneu-

Q   C.B.B.

monia in this way on the Solway marshes. What astonished me was the rapidity of its onset. One moment I was perfectly well and another I was feeling like nothing on earth and making tracks for home.

Unfortunately on the night in question there was a thick fog and for hours I could not find my way back across the marshes. The best way is to walk gently and easily and not over exert the body.

All these tips are for older men; youngsters seem to be able to 'take anything'. The fact remains that wildfowling calls for considerable powers of endurance and a sound constitution. It is no game for weaklings.

On such a night as this it is a crime to talk, one simply wanders along at an easy pace, pausing ever and again to listen to the various noises of the night.

There are many owls along this bank, they hoot on all sides, and now and again their dark shapes glide away over the fields. Far in the distance a train is puffing across the Carse, all sounds are amazingly clear on a frosty night. Very rarely will you find any wind in a great frost, all is deathly still. Standing here by the little stream with only your own shadow and dog for company one gets the sense of intense loneliness. There is nobody about at this hour, indeed it is a lonely place at the best of times. Perhaps you will meet the keeper, but it is unlikely. On such a night he will be within his cosy house. We have had many chats, he is a decent enough fellow, though not interested in geese or ducks so much as pheasants. He knows I have permission to shoot on the land around here and can give me many useful tips.

Some of these oak trees still retain their leaves, especially those trees which grow a little way down the bank; seen in the moonlight one at first mistakes the shrivelled blobs of

the dead leaves for roosting starlings. The latter birds however are down in the tall reeds.

At sunset, had you been standing on the bank higher up
the river, you would have heard the 'swish' of the passing
flocks going down to the tall reed beds. For half an hour at
the sun's setting they pass in companies and groups, all
flying in the same direction. The sound of the passage of
their wings is not unlike a passing gust of wind; sometimes
there is a curious musical whistle, this is a bird which has
some of its flight feathers missing.

There is no wind tonight to rustle the tall straight stems
of the plumed reed beds, they are picked out in a white
filigree of frost.

At last the path broadens out into a wide swathe, gently
dipping down towards the foot of the bank. There is
another burn here, a large stream which is very noisy in the
quiet. Slabs of thick ice are piled around it, some of the
slabs forming sugary shelves over the spring. A mallard
rises and for an instant its shape is seen against the pale
greenish sky but is soon lost. It is not a good night for
shooting, there should be more cloud.

A fence is visible now, half hidden by the reeds. This
marks the commencement of the groin and a few steps
bring the whole length of it into view. It is like looking
down a narrow passage, for the tall reed beds come right up
to the foot of the wall. At the end there is a bright spot
which marks the open river.

On setting foot on the stones it is immediately apparent
that ice has formed in a thin skin and great care is necessary.
It does not matter here, at the foot of the bank, for the reeds
grow in fairly firm and peaty soil but farther out, beyond
the reeds, a slip might be serious. The labrador comes behind, skidding like her master on the slippery stones.

It seems to take a long time to walk down the long wall,

and here and there one has to wade across mud which happily is now frozen as hard as rock. This is where a breach has been made by the tide and the force of the water has rolled away the heavy blocks.

Even without ice and frost, walking along the top of the groin is by no means easy, for it is not flat on the top but rounded, becoming gradually narrower as one advances.

At last however the end of the reed beds is reached and there in front is the wide river, the far hills on the opposite shore cloaked in a white mist. It is a mile or two across at this point, a mile of treacherous sandbanks and swift currents. The farther we can get out on the groin the better it will be. At the very extremity there is a hollow place in the stones which will form a good hiding place for the gunner. There is a chance that on such a night graylags and pinks will fly over the end of the groin. It will mean a cold plunge for the labrador but she will go through hell to get a goose.

The ice comes up to the stones on either hand however, and it might be dangerous work if I dropped a goose out in the river. The dog might break through the ice and wear herself out in her struggles to regain the groin. This is a thing one must be extremely careful about when shooting with a keen dog on an icebound river. Near the end of the breakwater the tide has piled loose cakes of ice. Some are as big across as a table top, others no larger than dinner plates. As the tide recedes these chunks and slabs are left behind, piled one upon another, and there is a continuous grinding and clashing which sounds very loud in the quiet of the night. Spreading a sack in the hollow in the stones and placing an armful of dead reeds on top of it I sit down to wait. The tide is making and the ice floes crunch gently against the stone wall, rising higher and higher so that soon, by stretching out my gun barrel, I could touch them.

Overhead is the clear-cut moon, shining serenely, casting a black and horned shadow from myself across the stones. There is an open space of water close at hand and in this space the moon is reflected, distorted and broken by the rocking of the ripples. The reflection seems to be made of some treacly substance, for now and again little oblongs of light break away from the main reflection and then fly back again.

Geese had been croaking out on the river as we came down the wall, but now all is still save for the faint 'crunch, crunch' of the ice floes.

From time to time loud reports break the tense silence as the water in the main gutters rises under the skin of the ice. All along the length of the channels these cracks and bangs are sounding; one gets the sense of the mighty power of the tide which will not be bound or restrained even by the grip of the bitter frost. One calls to mind the descriptions by Polar explorers who hear this cannonade, on a much magnified scale, during the long Arctic nights. The slabs of thick ice are split asunder as wood is riven by the woodman's wedge; the swelling breast of the tide bursts its icy chains with scorn.

Charles is back on the fringe of the reeds; he will be able to cover that end of the groin in case an odd goose or two follows up the edge of the reeds.

After half an hour one begins to feel the stealthy gripe of the frost. It begins in the thighs, a numbing cold. Yet now I hear greylags croaking in the mists opposite and it may be I shall get a shot.

The sounds grow louder and soon, half hidden in the white vapour, a line of specks are seen, swimming in on the tide. But they do not come near the groin, they drift down the river. A mallard or two whistles over and all at once there is a sudden rushing sound which comes from the left and passes swiftly overhead. Nothing can be seen. It was caused by a flock of waders, redshank or dunlin perhaps.

Higher up the river there is an outburst of goose croaks and one old gander calls incessantly 'Cacack-cak-cack, Cacack-cack,' like an old farmyard goose.

It is interesting to note here, with regard to greylag geese, that they are less noisy than the 'pinks'.

There is an hour or two before dawn when wild geese (like humans) sleep very soundly and at such times are absolutely silent. I recently had a good instance of this. One extremely bitter January morning I made my way out through the reeds to the edge of a wide gutter.

The night before I had seen greylags frequenting this part of the shore and expected to get a shot as soon as dawn broke.

My labrador felt the cold and shivered violently all the while, and indeed it was one of the coldest nights I ever remember. After a long time dawn began to break over the hills and wildfowl were heard on the move, but no geese.

Two mallard flew past the gutter and I dropped the drake (a beauty) on the other side, the labrador having to swim across to retrieve it. But at the shot quite twenty greys 'lifted' out of the short reeds behind me and went to sea! I had made a considerable noise going out through the frozen reeds close to them, yet they had not stirred or even croaked!

But to return to my description of the moonlit river. A faint sound behind me makes me turn about and there, sixty yards or so up river, a dark shape is seen on the water. Is it some stump of a tree, some piece of wreckage coming up on the tide?

As it draws slowly nearer I strain my eyes to make out its precise shape. As I watch, a blaze of orange flame leaps from its bow and a shattering roar breaks the stillness. The echoes go tumbling over one another, to re-echo again and again from every recess and corry in the hills.

Out on the river is a desperate flapping as a wounded goose beats the water with its wings. The labrador shivers violently and seems to wish to plunge into the icy water.

The dark shape now discloses itself as a gunning punt. The puntsman has come up on the tide and has managed to creep upon a gaggle of geese out in mid-river. From all sides there comes a great outcry, as party after party of geese take wing, some going inland and others away down river towards the sand banks.

It is of little use waiting now, for it will be hours before they are back again, so there is nothing for it but to retrace one's steps down the slippery breakwater, picking up Charles en route.

Here an accident happens which might well have proved a tragedy. The labrador slips on the stones and falls into the river among the ice floes. Desperately she tries to regain a foothold on the slabs. She can get her forepaws on to the edge of one slab, but as soon as she endeavours to raise herself she slips back under the water. Luckily she is close to the reeds and Charles, seeing the situation, gallantly plunges in. The mud is rotten and unfrozen under the skin of ice and he breaks through, going in to above his knees. But he gets the dog by the collar and hauls her out and manages to get out himself, with a helping hand, from the groin.

And so home, back along the frosty track through the silent trees and the ultimate warmth and cosiness of the patient little car standing in the black shadow of the barn.

So ended a most enjoyable moonlight adventure.

In a former book (*The Sportsman's Bedside Book*) I described many visits I had after pigeons in a spinney named

Wildwood. Of all the woods I have known Wildwood is my favourite, and though I now live farther away I am still within reach of it. It has grown up a good deal since the *Bedside Book* days, the firs are taller, so much so that they no longer afford good cover for the ambushed gunner.

These trees were planted close together to form a warm cover for foxes (it is in the heart of the Pytchley country) and they are still thick and green at their tops, but as is the habit of the species, the lower branches have died. When the trees are small they form a cosy retreat for all manner of wild animals, but when they attain their twentieth year or so most of the cover has 'gone up aloft' and foxes do not like it so well.

I think Wildwood interests me so much because of the many kinds of trees which grow there and also because it is planted on a hill above a pool.

A wood which is planted on undulating ground is vastly more interesting than a 'flat' wood, that is, a wood planted on level ground.

The other evening I paid Wildwood a visit. The leaves were nearly all off the trees, but the big oak in the very centre still retained most of its foliage, though the leaves were bleached to the colour of new leather. All day the weather had been cold, a bright, frosty, gem of a day. As I walked up the ride there was white rime on the grass and on the brambles by the side of the path. On this reverse slope the rays of the sun had been unable to reach the frozen ground, the white rime had been there the whole day.

On the right-hand side of the path there was a thick carpet of brambles. Some of the leaves were a bright green (brambles seem to retain green leaves until the spring), whilst others were a beautiful deep rose pink. A rabbit scurried under the arching spined branches and he was

A Wildwood Rabbit

able to get away without once becoming visible, only the shaking of the leaves and a rustling told of his flight.

Rabbits love lying out under bramble brakes. These woodland rabbits have different habits from their field brethren and I fancy they are of a different colour and their fur of a much more greyish tinge. They have their holes in the bordering hedges and up under the firs where the bluebells grow. Sometimes when I have been lying perfectly still beneath the trees I have seen a rabbit hopping along among the ferns and dead leaves. When these woodland rabbits feel secure and are not suspicious of man, they take things in a very leisurely manner, hopping along slowly, dragging their pads with a curious gait and sniffing the ground with down-bent head, exactly like a tame rabbit let loose on the lawn. Sometimes too they will shake a pad behind them, though what the object of this action may be I cannot guess, unless it is to dislodge earth from between their toes.

Though they have burrows actually in the wood, under the trees, they spend the greater part of their daylight hours in the hollow ash stumps. These stumps, which are the original sites of the full grown trees, are deep rooted; when the 'poles' were cut down they languished awhile among the bluebells and then, still full of life deep down within their cores, they threw up young shoots which in themselves never attained any great size and were more in the nature of whippy 'wands'.

Where the main trunk was severed the weather eats its way in, hollowing out the interior. Bright green moss grows thickly round the cavities, within it is warm and snug. The rabbits make their homes there and in winter, especially when snow lies on the woodland floor, covering all with a thick soft blanket of white, they seem to prefer these hollow 'tumps' to their holes in the earth. They will have one or more bolt holes, but these retreats may often prove death traps, for the poacher with his keen-nosed lurcher will find them out, and having no means of escape the rabbits are easy prey.

I noticed a movement in the top of a tall oak on the right of the path. It was a grey squirrel, and as I watched it swung from one tree to another, skilfully gripping a hanging branch. Sometimes a squirrel will fall whilst 'changing' from tree to tree but this very rarely occurs and I have only seen it happen once.

The red squirrel is seen no longer in our midland woods and the reason for its disappearance is mysterious. It may be something to do with the 'grey' or it may be the little owl. A naturalist once told me that he had seen a little owl pluck a red squirrel off a branch and kill it. Now, in this part of the world, the red squirrel is as rare as a polecat or a pine marten.

The last one I saw was in Dumfriesshire and I fear I killed it, quite by accident. I was motoring down a road and it ran across under the wheels. To kill so cunning and agile a little creature as a red squirrel by running over it in a car must be an uncommon occurrence.

A gaudy jay flew into the green fir tassels as I reached the top of the ride. They are common in Wildwood for I do not shoot them, though they are mischievous brutes and do an excessive amount of damage to pheasant and partridge chicks, to say nothing of the more important (at least to my idea) wild bird fledglings.

I went in quietly under the pines. Lying among the moist red leaves I saw some faded cartridge cases and they brought back memories of last year's pigeon shooting.

All through the long hot summer they have lain there, and I thought of the many fragrant summer dawns, when all the woodland birds were singing, and I had not been standing under the pines to see, and hear, and smell. I had been in my bed at home, between four walls, or attending to my daily round of duties, missing all these lovely things. I am so greedy for life outdoors that I grudge every moment spent under a roof. I love the woods and the fresh air as much as Jefferies worshipped the sunshine. I love the sunshine but too much of it wearies me; I could never live in a hot country.

To my mind our climate is perfect. To one who can roam the woods and fields, the soft grey days which we may expect in November and April are as lovely in their way as the sunny days of summer.

There are windless afternoons in April when the sun is hidden and the sky softly luminous. The trees and hedges, clad in their clean new green are lovely, the tips of the half opened larch buds are without movement. Everywhere all is so new and fresh; perhaps a gentle rain is pattering, bringing out all the sweetness of the earth. The mating call of the chaffinch is constant, 'rip, rip, rip,' it sounds on all sides, along the hedgerow, in the woods. Blackbirds warble from valley to valley, their song dominates all. They love the soft rain and promise of the green paradise which will soon be theirs, renovated and so lusciously luxuriant.

It is the memory of these soft grey days, when the hedges are dripping and distances blue, which tears at the heart of the Englishman in distant countries where the sun is always shining. And when we do get our quota of sun we are glad of it.

Lying thus in the woods and keeping perfectly still it was interesting to listen to all the country sounds. At such times I have imagined myself blind, only able to form mental pictures from the multitude of noises which my ears telegraphed to the brain. It takes a considerable time to sort each sound and 'pigeon hole' it with an appropriate picture.

First a cow is heard mooing in a distant pasture, then the 'cruik' of a moorhen on the square pond below the wood, and far in the background the musical shrillings of children at play. After a great deal of practice I could tell you not only the time of day but approximately the time of year. It would be much more difficult in May when so many birds are singing and the continuous wild music would drown most other sounds.

Baby Chaffinch

A carrion crow caws three times and a 'tap tap' tells of a fence post being driven into the ground. The clucking of a delighted hen which has just deposited an egg up at the Manor farm, presents an easy picture. The farm is fully half a mile away, perhaps even more; it is amazing how sounds carry and the voice of the domestic hen is peculiarly penetrating. The barking of a dog (a very usual accompaniment to rural noises) was not often absent. This particular sound carries as far as any and on a still night I have heard it from well over two miles.

The infinitesimal 'tweet' of hunting tits is always heard in the woods; these birds are in the firs yonder. The soft clap of a landing pigeon sounds ever and again from the ash poles. It is difficult for these rather ungainly birds to alight without sound, their wings strike the branches smartly. This 'clap' is not the same sound as the striking of wings over the pigeon's back, which is a feature of the courtship flight. In springtime and early summer they swoop upwards, bringing their wings together over the back and then beat them rapidly on the downward swoop, gliding again as they soar.

The tame pigeons, the white fantails at the Manor farm, have an exaggerated edition of the wild pigeon's play, though in their case it is not confined to courtship.

Not very many wild birds glide. I used to watch the starlings in the meads, and longed to be able to glide as they do. They sometimes travel over an entire field with rigid wings. Herons frequently glide long distances, their huge cupped vanes make ideal planes for the purpose. The finches and the thrush family never glide, the smaller the bird the harder it is for them. The study of birds' wings is an intensely interesting subject and one well worth thought.

The wings of sea birds are well adapted for gliding, and we see the albatross, king of gliders, has an enormous span, specially designed for effortless flight. As a general rule those 'land' birds which have short and rounded wings glide well, birds such as partridges, owls, pheasants, and sparrow-hawks are specially adapted. Some wings are suitable for flying in close cover, others (as in the case of the passerines) for 'general work'.

The noises of the night are of quite a different order and do not vary so much with seasonal change. Even in spring the night noises do not differ materially from those of midwinter. There is little bird song (save, in season, the nightingale and sedge warbler); one has to be a good naturalist to interpret the rustles and clicks and faint subdued whisperings which mostly belong to hunting animals in search of food. The Redskin so tutored himself in these matters that he became almost as perfect as an animal. To my mind his life was ideal; in constant touch with nature, a life of natural hunting in the woods; no wonder they had such noble faces and proud bearing and in their way were very religious. They were cruel perhaps, but less cruel than modern man, it was not so much cruelty as a scorn of physical pain.

I am afraid that this train of thought has led me away from Wildwood, so I must return thither and say more about the wood itself.

My mind went back over the year, to the time when the very first bluebell pierced the leaf mould; every day there would be more, until there was a whole carpet under the pines. Then the buds formed and at last the flowers burst forth in a sea of lavender blue, lit here and there by a shaft of sunlight as it pierced the fir branches. In the big oak the rooks would be busy, making the woodland ring with their cries, and then the cuckoo comes in the early morning, one with the fresh, cut-apple smell, of the spring dawn.

What a ringing of bird voices there must be in Green Wildwood on a May morning, yet nobody was there to listen, and smell the freshness of it all!

Slowly, slowly, the twigs would be hidden by the un-folding leaves, the rooks' nests would become less visible every day until they were quite hidden by the reddish leaves of the new oak. The sycamore saplings close by would unfold luscious, green, wide-spread fingers, through which the sun shaft glowed with a green fire.

Little by little then the bird song would cease, every morning there would be fewer birds singing and the rooks up

in the big oak were silenced. Down under the firs the bluebells were tired and old and the sea of blue a carpet of poddy
heads. Then followed the long, hot days when the sun tried
so hard to pierce the cool shade down here beneath the firs,
and the sweet perfumed evenings, when the honeysuckle
bushes made the air so sickly with their fragrance.

Fox and badger prowled here; my old friend clip-eared
Rufus with his lame leg; Brock's descendants, little spiny
people and wee furry folk, went about their business in the
shadowed aisles; Ben the owl, hooted overhead and Pipeete
the bat circled the pool. Nobody to see, nobody to care, too
busy with their bombings, and their sweat and blood and
misery. What meant the Epic of Dunkirk to Wildwood?
During those hot weeks it would be dreaming, green and
cool. Perhaps it is the Wildwoods we are fighting for, I hope
so, for I would fight for little else; these things I hold dear,
these places I worship.

And then one morning old man Autumn came stealing,
dew footed, with cobwebs and gossamer in his hair. He
stretched out a knotted finger and touched an oak leaf, it
tinged red, and the birds were silent.

Pigeons came for the acorns, and the proud and burn-
ished pheasant, walking sedately on pointed toes, be-
spurred like a smart officer of cavalry, hunted among the
dead leaves. The bright eyed blackbird, with his suit of jet,
turned over the damp leaves, in search of worms. Autumn
stalked on through the wood and in his wake there was a
faint misty aroma of decayed leaves which had all the spices
of the red woods in it.

Now for a short space I was here, standing under the trees
of my beloved Wildwood, looking at the sun, all golden
among a maze of glistening bare branches, settling down
over the park.

R   C.B.B.

Up in the tall aspen opposite the pigeons are coming in. For an hour before sunset they will come and sit and sit, not moving, making no sound, hunched with distended crops until their day's feed is digested and they drop down into the warm firs. Others wheel about, their wings spread in the sunlight. Soon winter will be here and the snow, and long starlight nights.

Just outside Wildwood, within a hundred yards, there is a huge hole in the slope of the green field. Brown earth is heaped around the edge, some giant has scooped it out with a stroke of his spiked club.

A German bomber came over here a month ago, in the afternoon. He dropped a bomb, a big bomb, why, only the Nazi mind can comprehend, for there is no house within a mile save a farm where the swallows make play about the outhouses.

He missed my Wildwood by a hundred yards and droned on to Germany. That bomb! I thought of it, of how the metal was obtained for it, how it was made in a distant factory in a distant country by a strange man I had never seen, of how it was loaded into the plane and carried all those miles across the sea and the white cliffs of Dover. Guns shot at the plane but missed it, people remarked on its passage. Nearer and nearer to Wildwood, my Wildwood, it came, then . . . 'Wheeeeeoo . . . Wham!' and there was that stupid hole in the damp turf where the green woodpeckers hunt for ants in April. All very futile and wearisome.

It is restful to watch the little birds preparing for the night, it will be warm and cosy under these green-tasselled coverlets.

A curious mist rolled between the trees, which smelt raw and damp, and there was only a glow now behind the wood.

The blackbirds were a-chinking and the pigeons had gone to the firs. I must go, go back to the four walls and my own kind. I envy the wild things their sweet dormitory and simple minds. They live in the sun and wind and are part of it, they are one with the heat and cold, the freshness of dawn, the quiet benediction of night.

Are we so sane? . . . I wonder.

Lambs

CHAPTER XII

Swallow's Nest

Chapter XII

The horsedrawn plough is rapidly being replaced by the Fordson, the hay and corn is no longer cut by hand; machinery does all these things. It takes the sheaves and binds them, it threshes the corn, it drills the furrows, and milks the cows, but the hedge is still cut by hand.

Of all the village characters the hedgecutter interests me most, I suppose because I am so in love with hedges. I like to see him work, bending the strong and whippy briars to his will, his large leather gauntlets proof against the sharpest thorn. This hedgelaying is a great art and as satisfactory in its way as ploughing, though infinitely slower.

Bill Dickens is aged sixty-nine, he looks seventy-nine. The weather has tanned and creased his skin but there is health in his clear grey eyes.

His hat is a classic. It is clay-coloured and conical, like a fruit pudding. It is a gem of a hat, up to now I have only seen it in a Rembrandt etching. I have seen it coming home in the frosty evening when the sky is salmon pink and flecked with gold clouds, I have seen it going down the road in front of me on a summer morning with a cuckoo shouting just over the hedge, I have seen it when the snow has whitened it . . . truly a classic hat.

Bill seems to wear a sack round his waist at all seasons, even on the hottest day. He knows as much about a hedge as the little red mice, almost.

I don't know how many prizes he has won at the Hunt Competitions. He can turn his hand to most jobs around the farm, from delivering a calf to 'muck spreadin', but it is at hedge laying that he excels. He has not been a farm labourer all his life. When he was a young man he worked in the coal mines in the Black Country close to Wolverhampton.

He told me the true tale of the Seven Whistlers and my flesh crept accordingly. Here it is, though I am not going to put it into dialect form, partly because I am not clever enough, and because dialect is sometimes wearisome for the average reader.

There used to be a very fine brass band at the colliery where he worked. It was famed far and wide for its skill, volume and artistry.

One night there was a fall in the workings, the band was

there entombed. Not a man escaped. Bill was in the mine at the time, he was just lucky, that's all, as were many other of his mates. The tragedy was not surprising, because the morning before, the sleeping miners in their grey little houses in a wet straight street had been wakened in the early hours by the Seven Whistlers. No man could explain the Seven Whistlers, but whenever there was to be an accident in the pit they were heard, seven whistles in the black night, under the grimy windows.

Some months after the accident, when the bodies had been brought out of the very womb of the earth, Bill was working with his mates at the 'face', near the old disused workings where his pals had died.

Suddenly Jim Coleridge laid down his pick and put a hand on Bill's arm.

'Listen, Bill,' he said. Bill listened. From far away in the old workings came the strains of the Colliery Band, the thump of the drum and deep tones of the big brass. 'D'you hear it, Bill?'

'Aye I hear it, Jim, I ain't a'going to work in the mine no more. I'm going up above, on to the land. The Seven Whistlers won't ever whistle fer me.'

So Bill left the mine and came to the fields and God's good air, to the frosty hedges and his ringing bill. There is not a hedge that he does not know about here, he has laid most of them in his time.

He married soon after he left the pit and they had first a son, who was apprenticed to a wheelwright, then a daughter, an ugly wench if ever there was one, who surprised the whole village by marrying a stockbroker's clerk. A good match for Ivy, she was proud of her catch.

'A mint o' money her 'usband had,' Bill told me, 'as nice a gentleman as you could wish to meet. I told him, when he asked me if he might marry me darter, I said, "Ivy's not good enough for a fine gentleman like you." But he only laughed and said 'e wanted her, that 'e loved her. So they married and they've been 'appy enough. A good girl was Ivy, not much to look at, not what you might call a beauty, but a good girl.'

There was a proper 'do' at the village hall and the bridegroom's parents were there, fine folk in a big car. They sat in the pub garden after the wedding and seemed unhappy. Perhaps they thought their son had married beneath him, but it was none of their business.

As long as the young folk were happy it wasn't their concern. Bill's wife died five years ago and he was left all alone, with a woman to 'do' for him. Life is a bit grey now, but somehow he carries on. I believe he takes a supreme joy in working in the wild weather, bending the thorns, weaving them without effort.

On his face are scars from old battles with the hedge; sometimes, for all his watchfulness, a slashing thorn-shod whip springs back and cuts him until the blood runs.

I must not forget his dog. Bingo is lean and black with crop ears, he is old, sixteen years so Bill tells me; a wonderful dog.

Bill does not always work at the same place or on the same farm, but Bingo always knows where to track his master. Bingo is rheumaticky and does not like getting up early in the morning; he wisely prefers the cottage fire and the rug made of coloured scraps before the glowing bars, where the big black kettle hisses, crusted with wear like an old boiler engine.

At noon Bingo is off in search of his lord, he goes straight to the place where the old man is working. Nobody knows how or why the dog can tell where his master has gone. Bill always tells him before he leaves where to come and find him. Before the day's work is over Bingo is in his old place, curled up on his master's jacket, or on the rush basket if it is cold weather and Bill keeps his jacket on.

Yes, a wonderful dog is Bingo and a hero of many a bloody fight. Like his master he is scarred. He never lets anyone stroke him, not even Bill. His hackles rise and he grumbles thunder grumbles, as a polite warning. If the warning is ignored Bingo bites and no half measures about it.

Soon he will die and then perhaps the old man will die too, for Bingo is all he has left to remind him of his sunnier days.

There is another character in the village who deserves mention, Brickett my keeper.

When I took a small shoot in the locality, principally to help out with the rationing, for there is nothing on it save multitudes of rabbits, I cast around for a man to look after it for me. Brickett was recommended and I took him on. He had been a keeper on a big estate and is quite one of the old school. He is a typical keeper in appearance, of middle height with what I call a fiery face and a truculent blue eye. He wears a wide skirted coat of antique cut with big hare pockets. This coat belongs to his earlier life, of big woods, pheasant pens and winter shoots, a life which is fast disappearing. He pursues the so-called 'sport' of rabbit catching with a peculiar intensity and perseverance, reminding me of a terrier.

He has three ferrets, all extremely bad workers, but he looks after them well and feeds them regularly; some say he thinks more of his ferrets than he does of his wife, indeed it is whispered in the village that he beats his wife on occasion, but only in his cups.

I shot a good many rabbits early on in the season by walking round, but now there is no cover in the hedges and

none on the fields, so Brickett has to ferret them, a 'sport'
I loathe for it is a cad's sport. Yet it is the only way to get
these rabbits out. The largest warren, Crow Wood, is a
steep bank which was once the site of an ancient mon-
astery. The bank is honeycombed with holes all along its
length and once a ferret gets in these burrows it is gone
for hours.

The most usual view I have of Brickett is a stern view,
with his head down a hole calling to his ferret or listening
for a rabbit. No matter how cold the wind he grubs among
the red earth, his hands caked with it, impervious to frost,
as keen and hard as an old lurcher.

He ties sacking round his knees for 'kneelers', he never
wears a top coat, though in really wet weather he dons a
tattered 'mac'. His ferrets never bite him (at least so he says)
because he feeds them 'in the dark'.

He remembers fights with poachers in the old days and
how one moonlight night, by the big plantation, he and his
father who was the head-keeper, and another under-keeper,
set about a gang of roughs who were after the pheasants.
He was only a lad and soon got knocked out. He rolled into
the ditch and lay there trembling. He saw a big man go for
his father with the stock of a gun, but down came the good
old ash plant on the fellow's head.

'Lor bless you sir it wur a tarrible blow me father give 'im,
the chap just crumpled up on the ground with his 'ead
split open. I knew me father 'ad 'it too 'ard, but if 'e 'adnt,
it would 'ave bin 'im that 'ad the cracked skull. The man
was dead sure enough with 'is skull stove in, same as an egg
shell.'

Soon after I engaged Brickett rumour got busy. Two
people told me that he was a poacher, the worst in the
village. I did not care if the report was true, as many of the
best keepers have been poachers at one time or another (I

am speaking of the very rural villages), but I did not believe them.

Not long ago I went alone to my shoot after a duck. It was a wild and windy evening and they were coming well. I heard a shot from over the hedge and a brown lurcher dog ran through, on the heels of a wounded rabbit. It caught it and went back through the hedge with it in his mouth. Then came a figure through the dusk. It was Brickett. He did not see me under the shadow of the thorns.

Brickett is a Section Leader in the Home Guard, and a very efficient one. I forgot to mention that he saw service in the last war and was wounded twice. The other Sunday he did not turn up on parade as usual and there was one other absentee, a pimply youth who works for Major Howard at the manor farm.

The sequel came later. Apparently Brickett had been suspicious for some weeks past at the continued absence of Willie Wilson, and had taken the morning off to walk round the shoot. He had caught Willie red handed with two rabbits and a ferret, a very awkward position for everyone concerned, for Willie was in his section. Still, in a village, these things will happen.

Our Home Guard is good 'as Home Guards go', for we have a genial commander and a high percentage of old soldiers who know their job. When we turn out on parade we certainly are a fine body of men, there's no denying it. The mainstay of the whole organization is Dukes, ex-sergeant major of the Guards. He is the corner post, without him we should be like sheep without a shepherd.

Dukes has a 'voice', in addition to many other accomplishments, and our social meetings are considerably enlivened by his fine baritone. Dukes really can perform, for as a boy he sang solo in a cathedral choir in the east country.

During the summer evenings we drill in the parson's meadow, and the cows gather round in an interested circle with shocked surprise in their mild eyes.

Ferreting and wildfowling is comparable to coarse fishing and salmon fishing, the former respective 'sports' are without the true sporting flavour and necessary skill.

Yet ferreting is THE pastime of the average villager and they think highly of it. Every Saturday afternoon, and Sundays as well, they may be seen cycling off with the ferret box strapped on the back.

Boxing Day in the country is always set aside for ferreting —it is as important a date in the Rural Calendar as the 12th

Stoat

of August is to the 'quality'. Everyone who has a gun and a couple of ferrets is off at the crack of dawn; fair weather or foul, it matters not.

I always think that ferrets are obscene looking creatures with their snake like bodies and pink eyes; they cannot be compared to the wild ferrets, the stoat and the weasel. Bloodthirsty as these little gentlemen in brown may be, they are mighty hunters and ferociously brave. It has been said that if the stoat was as large as a lynx it would be one of the most dangerous animals alive and there is truth in the statement. They are also beautiful in appearance and have not the pale and cruel eyes of the ferret. It has never been my good fortune to see a hunting pack of stoats, though I have come across many instances of it. Nearly every hedger has seen a pack, but I always suspect that it is a family party on the prowl, for the dam will teach her young to hunt as a vixen tutors her cubs.

We occasionally find a white stoat in this part of the country, though not a true albino for the eyes do not change. In the North of Scotland, of course, the stoats always change colour, and I remember seeing a fine specimen near Montrose basin. My chief 'grouse' against stoats is that they do an enormous amount of damage to wild bird fledglings. As to their chief quarry, the rabbit, I have little sympathy for the creature. They are cowardly and destructive beasts and poison the pastures. The grass round a big warren is nearly always withered and yellow, and sheep will not feed where rabbits have been. The stoat seems almost as much at home up in the hedge top as on terra firma and there are few nests, built in the thorns, which he cannot reach. If he finds a nestful of baby birds he will wolf the lot and then curl round and go to sleep in the nest.

In this and the adjoining county there are many deserted lanes, old roads which have long since been disused and have gone back to nature. One I have in mind, Carval's Lane, is not far from my home. I frequently ride or walk that way, a charming subject indeed for the naturalist or artist, and in the autumn, when the acorns are ripe, pheasants hunt the ditches and woodcock come to the little spinney half-way along its length. Looking at this old road, one can form a good picture of what might happen if mankind were to be wiped out of England and nature come into its own again.

The bordering hedges spread out and out across the sward, the blackthorn sends forth its tap roots, the dense thickets advance to meet each other.

Grass covers the lanes in a few years, though on tarmac it takes considerably longer. First the floods of winter and the fierce frosts crack the surface in dozens of places, weeds and grass find a foothold. The gutters, no longer kept clear, become choked and the earth is washed from the grass verge over the smooth surface. This would in turn be thick with weeds and as each summer the sward advances, the creeping plants of clover and trefoil, hare's ear, dandelion and thistle, help to swell the tide.

At last the road is hidden and the hedges, meeting, form a solid winding thicket for miles. Each hedge in time grows a line of trees, or more properly a wall, for with no billhook to lay them low they could flourish and reach maturity. Birds and mice would be constantly sowing seeds of more trees, so that the fields in time become crossed and bisected with lines of timber.

The thorn hedges grow higher and form trees also, and after a very long while the fields themselves become studded with trees and bushes.

Only the downs and the hills and high ground remain unchanged. The low lying plains, the valleys and hollows, become a jungle as they were in early times. It is fascinating to imagine Britain 'gone wild'.

Walking up Carval's Lane the other day I built up a picture such as I have described. I imagined that in one instant of time man was swept away as if he had never been. In the great cities men would be taken, whatever they chanced to be doing, snuffed out by the hand of some Magician, or Deity, who was disgusted with what man had made of the gift of life. He would say :

'See, Man professes to be so in love with Life yet he destroys his brother, he murders little children and lays the cities in smoking ruins. Man, who prides himself on being civilized! I will make an end of him, now in this very second, let him vanish from the earth. It seems that My experiment was a failure. I gave him a mind above the animals, I gave him free will. He has abused it. Selfishness and greed are the main causes. Enough, let him be removed.'

So man would vanish in the twinkling of an eye. In an instant—chaos, to be succeeded by sweet calm. Cars, bereft of drivers, career drunkenly onwards to pile and crash in the city streets. The big turbines continue to hum for a while and then sink to silence. Aeroplanes swoop earthwards, trains hurtle onwards, oblivious of the warning signals (so empty now) to crash against other trains or jump the rails.

The big ships forge ahead until their engines die. Some drift helplessly until they go ashore on the rocks, others collide and sink, some remain for years idly drifting, red with rust and white with gull droppings.

Millions of unfinished meals are left on plates, houses crumble in silence to the dust, to be swallowed by the green tide of tree and sward.

For a few dreadful days beasts and domestic animals confined in stables and four walls make hideous moans. Poor cows, standing patiently for the milkman to appear, fall ill with milk fever and die, their bellowings of pain fill the air.

Dogs run wild, killing the poultry. In a very short time domestic birds disappear. With the losing of the power of flight they could no longer survive.

Those beasts other than milking cows which were in the fields find sustenance, though there would be periods of starvation in bad weather.

Before many years have passed the fens become really fens again, for the dykes and drains are choked.

And this Deity, or Magician, which I have imagined, might say:

'Now let one single man return to this England, knowing what it used to be. Let him wander in the cities and the country and see what I have done with it."

I imagined that I was that unfortunate.

I would go first to the great cities. Here, after three hundred years, there would still be a wilderness of brick and stone. Here and there are the outposts of the green earth covering, trees and weeds and bushes. But it is a harder struggle for the plants and green things among so much cement, stone, and brick.

The weather would have got into the houses, into the great buildings, the streets choked by rusty iron and fallen rubble, the fine palaces and mansions windowless but still erect. There would still be precious stones and jewels in the jewellers' windows, in my lady's boudoir, and in the strong rooms of the Banks, heaps of useless gold.

Many houses show destruction by fire—for fires unattended would have spread—their blackened shells completing the hideous scene of desolation and horror.

Gladly would I go to the country, to be away from the signs of man. Yet even here, again and again I should come upon signs of that former civilization; the silent hamlet, hedged round with trees and bushes, the rusty metals of the railway lines across the bridges, and somewhat pathetically, roses and other 'domestic' flowers still blooming among the weeds.

In stable and yard lie piles of whitening bones, of cattle, horses, and pigs. The latter, if out in the fields at the time of the catastrophe, would rapidly go back to their wild state, running wild in the woods as their forebears did in the early times.

Richard Jefferies endeavoured to picture all this in *After London* and succeeds tolerably well. It is a fascinating subject.

Deserted roads, which first gave rise to these thoughts in my mind, are much beloved by certain species of birds. Redstarts have a particular liking for them. Every summer there are two pairs down Carval's Lane and they build in the knotted ivy creepers which embrace the big ash trees. The cock bird is a handsome fellow with the white spot, like a caste mark, on the forehead, and his rusty ever-trembling tail betrays his anxiety. His alarm note, 'Uee, Uee, tic, tic, tic', sounds long before you are near the tree. On the 'tic, tic, tic' of his alarm the tail vibrates rapidly sideways. He waits until you are close and then dips swiftly, showing the rusty tail, to the next tree. The nest is difficult to find and the hen sits closely. Nightingales, too, frequent the lane, but they do not breed there. Curiously enough they prefer the coppices and spinneys bordering roads for, like the robin to which family they belong, the nightingale likes human company and noise.

The garden warbler, much more retiring, breeds in the thick underwood of the lane hedge. It is a stoutly built warbler not unlike the nightingale in colouring.

Whitethroats are regular summer visitors, greenfinches and chaffinches are common. The greenfinches have a particular liking for the elder bushes, and in the evening their twanging tropical song reminds one of some gaily painted canary.

The typical bird is the bullfinch. Six or seven pairs build every year in the blackthorn bushes, and the white dipping spot of white above the tail is a familiar sight as the cock and hen swerve along the hedgeside. On a hot afternoon in July the meadow browns bob over the thistles, millions of them, as far as one can see. And one day, near the big elms at the top of the lane, I saw a large tortoiseshell, a rare butterfly in this part of the world.

Over the bramble bushes dart the thick-bodied dragonflies, fearsome beasts known to the rustics as 'hornets'. Some are a beautiful rich blue, others reddish brown, their fat bodies as broad as one's thumb.

It is in autumn that the lane is most beautiful, when the oaks have turned and the brambles are rose-red, at the time of the fieldfare and the redwing. 'Chek chek chek', they pass over against the golden haze, and some dive down into the tops of the ashes where they sit upright with heads turning as they scan the surrounding fields.

A family of long-tailed tits passes along the hedge; they will hunt along its entire length and are great travellers, wandering over miles of country in a single day.

In the now bare thorns is seen the flimsy platform of a dove's nest. It is not so substantial as that of the wood-pigeon, the architect is now far away in the sunny lands of Spain and Africa.

Though birds are fond of these lanes they will sometimes shun certain localities and the reason for this is not obvious. I know several remote hedgerows which have been allowed to run riot and many grass-grown tracks bordered by dense bushes which are entirely devoid of bird life. Any lane with a southern aspect, provided it is sheltered, is favoured, but those on the high ground, and which are open to the winds, are very often avoided.

I knew a lane in Wiltshire, only two hundred yards long, which was so thick with nests that there was one in practically every bush; cirl buntings, hedge sparrows, red-backed shrikes, and a yellow-hammer's nest which, I remember, contained a cuckoo's egg.

The coombes on the downs, where the thorn bushes grow thickly, are highly favoured. This is quite understandable. These bushes, nicely sheltered, may be the only sanctuary for some miles and the only place where the birds can get out of the wind. As a general rule, nearly all the land birds, save the swallow family, hate wind, it blows their feathers the wrong way and knocks them about. Talking of swallows reminds me that some years ago I saw a perfect albino swallow. Albinism in the Hirundinidae is extremely rare, and I have never come across another instance of it. I saw this albino for two successive seasons.

Many a hot summer morning have I watched the swallows and martins collecting mud from the margin of a pond, which I used to frequent with great regularity.

Six willows grew on the bank and I hid behind one of them, and with my glasses could focus the busy little creatures within a foot or two.

Their most active time is between ten o'clock and midday on a hot June morning, before the sun has reached full power. During these two hours there was a never-ending stream of birds and at times the wet margin was a seething mass. They take such care to keep their tiny feet clean, especially their white under-tail coverts and wings. These are cocked up high, as a girl will lift her skirts above her knees. It took the martins about two minutes to collect the right amount of plaster, then away they went, twittering happily. Sometimes a newcomer would alight (for some reason) on another's back, occasionally two would fight each other.

Then one by one they ceased to come, they played instead in the upper sky, twittering and wheeling, glad to be done with the work for the day. For some reason most birds build their nests in the morning, most of the larger birds prefer the very early morning.

It has always amazed me the way that birds' nests withstand wild weather. Rooks' and herons' nests will last for years, so cunningly are they woven among the branches, and even the old nests of blackbirds and thrushes will stand for a couple of years and sometimes longer. One of the reasons is that, as they are built up in the hedge, the wind soon dries them (even in winter) and dried grass will last for ever, so it seems.

It is most interesting to watch a bird build its nest. Once the construction has got well under way the task is easier, it is the placing of those first few fibres which takes the time and skill. Even the frail basket of the bullfinch, which is almost invariably built of fine rootlets, will stand any amount of wind and weather. When the cup is formed the hen will get inside, standing almost on her bill and with tail straight up in the air, pushing with her thighs against the lining of the nest, at the same time turning round and round with a shuffling motion. It has never been my good fortune to watch a chaffinch or a goldfinch build its nest; the felting process is, I believe, different from the methods employed by thrush and blackbird.

The greatest mystery of all is how the nest of the wood-pigeon can hold together for more than a season. The ring-dove will not always build its nest of sticks. I have found it made of hay, built in a low alder bush. I have also found three pigeon's eggs in one nest, but whether or not they were laid by the same bird I do not know.

The reader, if he has manfully struggled thus far, will have guessed that certain aspects of the country attract me more than others, woods for instance, and streams.

Two other delights which deserve a chapter to themselves are field ponds and hedgerows. These subjects, studied intimately, are fascinating indeed. By field ponds I mean those natural ponds which are to be seen in nearly every county in England. The square artificial man-made 'pit' which is found in grazing country has little to attract, though even there, nature can sometimes make them beautiful.

The Field Pond

Such a natural pond I have in mind at the moment, within walking distance of this house.

It is set in some lonely fields on top of a high hill overlooking the Avon valley, a small affair as a typical field pond should be. It is hidden by rising ground but its presence is betrayed by the top of a willow, a very old tree, and several thorn bushes. It is most beautiful in early June when the hawthorn is out and the fields are ablaze with golden buttercups.

In shape it is almost a horseshoe and at one end the water shallows, where the cattle come to drink. Here the farmer has put a railing across, from one side to the other, to prevent his beasts from getting bogged in the deeper part. The fence was put up some years ago, for it is rotting and green; wasps love it and on any hot day in July and August they may be seen gathering 'paper', chewed wood pulp, with which they make their nests.

On the north and west sides of the pond there is a steep bank honeycombed with rabbit burrows. The brick-red earth has been scraped out into mounds which hide the lush grass and for some way out into the mead the grass is close clipped by the rabbits. Their worn runs are visible like paths, for a 'bunny', even when in a hurry, will usually go back to his hole by the same way. The old poacher studies these runs, setting his snares on the 'jumping' place.

If you look at a rabbit run you will see that it is not one continuous 'worn' path but a series of bald patches. The wild rabbit progresses in a series of hops.

The custom of rabbits to sit on any eminence is well known to poachers. Any ant hill or hillock shows evidence of sitting rabbits and sometimes a gin cunningly placed on the top will catch quite a few. I know a case where an old poacher made an artificial ant hill and caught large numbers of rabbits on it.

Growing on the north bank are the hawthorn bushes. They are very old trees, as old as the pond perhaps, though they would be sown in the first place by visiting birds. The bushes, or more properly, trees, lean out over the water, and in June the cocoanut smell of the white hawthorn blossom fills the hollow above the pond. The tiny round, white petals drop off into the water and form a band of white which drifts to and fro with every breath of wind. In the shallower water, near the cattle drinking-place, water crow-foot grows in a solid mass, the exquisite little flowers with their yellow centres make a solid carpet of snow. The foliage of the water crowfoot, or as it is better known, water daisy, is almost as beautiful as the flower. Its little round leaves remind one of the water lily, but they are toothed and irregular round the edges.

There are four hawthorn trees, and one ancient crab tree which grows at the end of the bank. Its blossom also is very lovely and it too drops its pink petals, maiden's blush petals, into the water. Later, in mellow October time, the red rabbit-scratched earth is covered in fallen crab fruit; a great waste it seems that all that harvest should lie there ungathered. In days of peace when sugar is no longer rationed, my wife and I will gather those wild apples; crab jelly is pleasant with jugged hare.

I would like to describe the colours in the hawthorn leaves, just before the time of the first hard frosts. They are as lovely as the white blossom, perhaps even more exquisite. But it is June now, the 'Queen of the Year'.

On the east side, the mead slopes down to the margin of the pond in a gentle slope, and no rabbits have drilled their burrows in it, they prefer the steep hawthorn-shaded bank. Under the tough iron-like roots they are more secure, as the visiting poacher has found. Many a good ferret has been lost under those friendly trees for the spade cannot cut the tough roots.

In the middle of the pond, that is, at the top of the horseshoe, is a little island. This is what makes the pond so attractive. It is covered with bright green grass and surrounded by deep water—four feet or more—and the rabbits cannot eat the grass. Growing on the island is a yew bush. This tree again must have been sown by the birds. Perhaps long ago a mistle thrush or a fieldfare dropped a pip, birds are excessively fond of yew berries though it is such a poisonous plant to cattle. Had it been growing on the bank the farmer would have soon cut it down but here, on the island, it is secure. Like the hawthorn trees its branches are spread over the water, shadowing it.

Every year a wild duck breeds on this island, right under the overhanging branches, against the reddish trunk. I wonder how many broods have been reared in that snug place; it is a paradise for the baby ducklings. On the island they are safe from foxes and stoats. When they get older they scud about among the water daisies like tiny striped torpedo boats.

Besides the mallard family there is a resident pair of moorhens. What the moorhen does not know about field ponds cannot be worth knowing! Every little pit in the fields, no matter how small, has its moorhen family. On this pond they, like the mallards, always build in the same spot, under the hawthorns on the north shore.

The nest, a bulky affair of reeds, sticks and weeds, is built with considerable skill on a sunken tree, a sapling hawthorn which never reached maturity. Perhaps the rabbits killed it and burrowed round its roots so that one autumn gale sent it over into the pond. The sooty youngsters, as beautiful in their way as the striped ducklings, must soon know every inch of their home. What a charming picture they make, swimming among the white water daisies! When all is quiet, the plaintive wheezy squeak of these little blackamoors is continuous.

At one end of the horseshoe, the left-hand leg, rushes grow thickly, but they do not encroach far into the pond because the water is too deep. They form a thick green forest, impenetrable and mysterious, and the blue jewels of the dragon flies daintily perch on the broad shiny sword blades, their fairy wings, each with a large purple spot at the end, cocked daintily over their backs. Sometimes I see tapestry-red dragon flies, but the blue are the most common.

Occasionally a very gorgeous little person visits the pond and perches on the hawthorn branch above the waterhen's nest. But the kingfisher does not stay long, for as far as I can see there are no fish in this deep and secret pond. There ought to be . . . some golden carp or other fairy-like fish. But I have seen nothing more exciting than 'pollywoggles' and, in early spring, the sight of one solid jelly-like mass of wriggling tadpoles is faintly disgusting. Like the British army, nature always does spend on such a lavish scale. Waste is not considered, the margin is very big and it needs to be.

On the west side grows the willow, a very ancient tree, perhaps the patriarch of the pond. It grows half on the bank, half in the water, and its roots make fairy caverns of bright red roots, and when the sun is shining, lighting up the mysterious depths, they may be seen far down under the surface.

How many millions of crab apples and hawthorn pips must be in the pond? Like the wireless comedian I say 'I wish I had as many shillings'!

A little owl builds in the willow, for there is a hollow in the top of it. The mystery is why it never takes the baby ducklings and the sooty moorhen chicks. The reason may be that it breeds a little later than the ducks and waterhens.

He is a bold, fine-looking little gentleman, very aristocratic and with wonderful eyes. In the February days, when the weather is mild, he sits on top of the willow stump above the dark hole which has seen so many of his sons and daughters safely launched, mewing plaintively like a cat. As one Suffolk labourer had it 'that lil'ole bud she went woo, woo, woo, like my old tom cat.' He is spotted and barred like a nightflying moth, a little beauty.

On very hot days the poor gad-demented cattle come lumbering to the pond for shade and relief. They stand beyond the rails, as far as they can go, swishing their tails, their half-shut eyes black with a crawling mass of loathsome flies. They remain there for hours on end until the burning rays wheel below the crest of the bank and the rabbits hop out into the golden mead.

Another visitor, a heron, sometimes comes sailing on set wings, spread like a dark cloak. Affrighted moorhens scurry, though he would not harm them. He stands in the shallow water by the cattle drink, his spear couched, his eye round and indignant like a peppery old gentleman's. Fat frogs (there are many in this pond) find their way into his portmanteau.

As the summer advances the water recedes, leaving a criss-cross of cracks in the mud which ultimately flake off in cakes and shales. No matter how dry the summer, however, I have never seen the pond empty, there is always a comforting peaty darkness of deep waters under the red willow roots. And in the winter, after continued rain, when the valley below is one long brimming lake alive with lapwings, my pond swells until the fence by the cattle drink is 'chin deep'. It flows over, and a silver thread bursts on to the bright green northern lip and flows down into the mead. Then the snipe come and nobody disturbs them.

Many other birds besides the heron come to this pond.

It is their regular drinking-place. In the early summer mornings the portly wood-pigeons clapper noisily in the willow and have a look around before dropping down to the marge. They are perfect in every detail, blue grey and pinkish bloomed, with coral feet and white trousers and a perfectly magnificent iridescent splash of green blue and white on either side of their necks. They dip their bills down deep and gulp like a horse; they do not sip like the little field finches, the gay-painted chaffinches and yellow-hammers.

Turtle doves come also in high summer, birds of Spain with soft voices and exquisite lines. They are not grey like the big woodies, oh dear no! they are rich chestnut on the back, striped like tabbies, and when they fly they show their white petticoats, snow white, a broad band all round the margin of the tail.

Rooks come, thirsty after their acorn feeds in the golden valley; the rascally carrion with the voice of the evil one and, strangely too, the big brown owls come here for a bath. Some aver that owls do not bathe. This is a gross libel, they are most cleanly birds, as an aristocrat should be.

In the bird world the aristocrats are, first and foremost, the falcons, then the eagles and hawks, then the owls. We follow down through the 'middle-class' birds, such as ducks and finches, to the vulgar starlings and sparrows. The rook by the way is definitely 'middle class'. I am not sure that the great crested grebes should not be classed with the aristo-crats of the bird world.

A very lovely visitor to the pond is the grey wagtail. They breed in the wide water meadows down in the valley, but an occasional bird will visit the pond, running about on twinkling feet about the margin of the cattle drink. Daffodil yellow and soft grey, a fairy bird in fairyland. Foxes come here sometimes, they drink in the pool under the starlight, they sniff about the rabbit warren in the summer dusk.

Moles, always thirsty creatures, have their workings out in the meadow, their runs are visible, leading to the water; a raised snake-like line in the turf where they have bored their runway under. Their true drinking run however is deep. The old mole trappers knew where to find these drinking runs, locating them with a pricker, and a trap set there would catch every mole for a mile around if there was no other water in the vicinity.

Such is this pond, one of many I know.

. . . .

There is a different order of fascination in a hedgerow. Most hedges are more beautiful—to my mind—in winter, when they can no longer keep their challenging secrets. I do not speak of the ragged hedges, though they are beautiful enough in their unkempt wildness, but of the ordinary common-or-garden roadside hedge which is old, perhaps seventy years or more, and has been laid and laid over a number of years.

A newly planted hedge is most unattractive, for it is without character. The small 'quicks' are planted at regular intervals, the ditch below is neatly spaded out ready for the floods of winter. Years go by, the quicks grow rapidly, are cut, and grow again. Then perhaps the hedge is neglected, for say six or seven years. It runs riot, nature gets a grip on it. Nature is untidy, she does not think in straight lines as we do.

All manner of weeds grow and the ground ivy begins to creep about the roots of the thorn.

In summer the hedge is so thick one cannot see through it, only on the wrong side (there is a thin side to a hedge as well as a thick) can one search for nests and even in a strong sun it is difficult to see them. The stout thorns grow stouter, they thrust up and try to be trees. If the hedge is still neglected they will succeed and gaps will appear. Masses of red berries afford good provender for the field-fares and redwings.

These tall hedges are also used for roosting-places by the handsome grey 'felts', as the fieldfares are called, and the village lads armed with a 'clap net' sometimes catch them on moonlight nights. The big thrushes are however very wary, and fly off before the birdcatchers can get within range. The blackbirds and thrushes are less suspicious and are easily caught.

In the old days the netting of birds was a common practice, the unfortunate victims being made into a vast, and I fear appetising, pudding.

The country yokel has other things now to occupy his leisure time and the stuffy cinema or the village dance-hall has greater attractions.

Then comes an earth-stained hedger one winter's day. With great skill he plys his bill and the fine, hopeful thorns sway and crash. The ash trees, oaks and elms which have been sown by birds and are as yet one with the hedge, fall also, they are bound down and woven in and out into the body of the hedgerow.

Big thorn stumps remain and the ground ivy grows up and over. The little creeping hedge mice come carrying berries, running in and out, their big bright eyes quick to see danger. They also climb the thorns and seek out last year's nests, blackbird, finch, and hedge-sparrow, and store their harvest within. Sometimes the winds tilt the old nests and the red berries, with their puckered skins, are spilled out into the ditch below. Through the tangle of horizontal branches fresh shoots rise upwards as do other trees, more ashes, oaks and elms, sown by birds. They grow straight up, charming 'sticks' which make small boys' mouths water, and they try to cut them down with their blunt pocket-knives, leaving them half-hacked through.

Shadows are under the laid branches; even in grey winter there is mystery beneath the old thorn roots; mice, rabbits and stoats have their runs in and out, for miles.

The ditch below is choked with all manner of wild plants, lords and ladies, hemlock, Queen Anne's lace. In season the latter makes a band of exquisite pinkish-white filigree all along the border of the hedge and road.

Rabbits drill their holes through and through, from one side of the hedge to the other, some have bolt holes out in the fields. But the rabbits are fond of sitting under the ivy-clad thorn roots, and the snuffling spaniel pushes them out in front of the waiting gun.

Millions of birds are hatched in these hedgerows, and in the nettles in the ditch the whitethroat slings its frail casket of dried hay from stem to stem, though the nest will not be truly slung like that of the reed warbler.

In the June days the whitethroat comes into his own, the roadside hedge is his kingdom. He rises to the top of the sea of green and tangled weed and sings his song from his silver swelling throat, then sinks again below the surface.

Up in the thickest part of the thorns the bullfinch broods, sitting patiently while the cars roar by. No longer are these country roads white with dust as in the old days, the surface is hard and smooth, iridescent with oil after rain, and with perspiring beads of glistening tar in the very hot weather. Silverweed thrives near the edge of the road, a dusty-looking lowly plant which is nevertheless as soft as a rabbit's ear. The wild campion grows in the ditch and the loosestrife, and most alluring of all, the crumbly meadow sweet, beloved of the long green and red beetles, scarabs set with gems.

When old autumn comes with his frosty scythe and lays

these wonders low, all secrets are made plain, or nearly all. You will see nests you never guessed were there and realize the hedge has kept its secret well. You can recognise many of the species by the nests. And here, under the dead stinging nettles, are some old discoloured scraps of partridge shells; another secret well kept by a friendly wilderness. Old man's beard riots over the hedge from top to bottom, again sown in the first place by birds, or maybe the seed was carried on the wind. The dog rose also make free, using the thorns as a 'help-me-up'.

In October the hedge is a riot of colour and the loveliest leaf is perhaps that of the field maple. Words cannot convey the intense yet delicate tints of the clear yellow leaves. It is a yellow which is hard to imitate in paint, indeed I doubt whether it can be matched by any colour on the artist's palette. The field maple has a very black stem which shows up the colour of the leaves to their fullest advantage, and where the hedge has been laid efficiently the bushes are very thick. The actual leaf is beautifully shaped and cut into five, toothed lobes which are always arranged in pairs, springing from either side of the branch exactly opposite each other. If the field maple is allowed to grow it will attain a height of thirty feet or more, but it is in a hedge bush that the rich yellow foliage is seen to the best advantage. This clear yellow colour is so intense that one sees it afar off, and when the sun shines through it the beauty is greater still; it seems as if the very leaves are incandescent. The frosts and winds soon weaken their hold and they flutter down, revealing the slender dark branches, and in a very short while the flaming yellow sinks from sight and the maple bushes become one with the more prosaic hawthorn. In many of the midland lanes the hedges are composed entirely of maple, just as in the Border country one finds the beech predominating.

When the leaves fall and the first really hard frost comes the hedge is, to my mind, the most beautiful. There are red berries a-down it; when seen from the road or meadow, along the hedgeside, there is a bloom of deep carmine, and the fog freezes on every twig, transforming it. Not one spine escapes, not one section of stalk or berry, all are crusted with fairy fronds, miniature trees in themselves, trees and ferns of ice crystals. On the sunny side, the frost may melt for a space at midday and the twigs, healthily red, shine wetly. But soon the fog comes down again and the white particles form rapidly.

From over the hedge, in the rimy field, the sound of quarrelling starlings is heard as they jump up in the air and fight with one another over non-existent morsels.

And then, in the short winter dusk, the birds come flocking to the close-bound thorns for sleep. The hedge takes them and keeps them, safely and warm, while the cold white moon wheels overhead, throwing shadows from the bare branches on bank and ditch. The ditch is full of water, ice now, an inch thick.

.   .   .   .

It is a strange thing why canal banks and railway banks are so favoured by birds and beasts and, I might add, butterflies.

In the case of butterflies it is perhaps more easily explained. On sloping railway embankments, especially those which face south, the grass is cut every year and multitudes of wild flowers have a chance to see the sun and thrive. They are not choked by bushes or weeds and the knife does not cut close enough to lay them low. In a sense these warm banks, always well drained, are like the downs which are open to the light and air, and small creeping plants such as thyme, trefoils, and scabious thrive.

Rabbits are very fond of such dry places and in many

T   C.B.B.

localities one sees quite big warrens, the tenants of which have grown accustomed to the roar of passing trains. Birds frequent railway banks as much as the rabbits, for two very good reasons. First perhaps they are attracted by the telegraph wires, which seem to appeal to the bird mind even more than branches or twigs for perching upon, and secondly, the long grassy slopes make ideal nesting-places, as do the close-cropped thorn hedges on either side of the rails. These thorn hedges are however being gradually replaced by fencing, for the hedge, if it is to keep its density, must be cut frequently and this is a costly business.

Three species of birds are most partial to railway embankments; the yellow-hammer, the whinchat, and the tree pipit. In some counties the lark and corn bunting are also found.

All these species are fond of perching on wires, though the corn bunting will only be found where the fields adjoining the railway are extensive and well cultivated. This particular bird is a secretive soul. The nest is one of the hardest to find; indeed it is one of the few nests of the commoner British birds which I have never found unaided. Its life appears to be spent upon the telegraph wires and it seems to have no time even for food. The 'cobby' drab bunting will sit immovable, jangling its note monotonously hour by hour. This song of the corn bunting is in reality most musical to my ear and has a peculiar wild 'open airness' which is strangely romantic.

The tree pipit finds in the railway bank the ideal nesting site, and as railway property is private and therefore undisturbed they can rear their well-concealed brood in safety. The whinchat I have already mentioned in an earlier chapter as a lover of railway banks, and the short stub-tailed bird is a familiar sight in this part of the world. Their nests are also well concealed and the parent birds exceedingly wary.

In passing I might add that the whinchat is most partial

to thistly pasture land. In the later summer weeks it perches on the thistle tops, flitting from one to another, uttering anxious cries if young are in the neighbourhood. I have only found the nest on three occasions.

For three years my brother and I lived in an old farm-house at Gordon Hill near Enfield. Those years were some of the happiest of my life. During the week we both worked hard though at widely different occupations, myself as an art student and my brother as a pupil of Gordon Perry.

But at the week-ends we used to pack up our lunch and go away into the woods and fields, staying out all day until the sun set. In the summer time this week-end ramble was looked forward to all our working hours. Ten years ago, Gordon Hill was quite rural and on the verge of very lovely country, even though it was so near London. Hertfordshire has a very attractive character and the heavily timbered countryside appealed to us. We did not go 'hiking'; these rambles were across fields and through woods, searching for butterflies and birds. 'Chaselands', the old house where we lived, was reputed to have once been a hunting-lodge in the forest and the glamour of the woodlands still remained in some mysterious way. During the June nights, when we slept with our windows thrown wide open, the nightingales sang in the orchard trees close to the farm. These birds were also common in the gardens of the nearby villas, though I never met anyone who realized the fact.

Not far from the house the Gordon Hill-Cuffley railway ran on a long embankment, to eventually pass over a very high viaduct. This railway bank was a fine place for butter-flies. In those days I knew more about birds than I did about insects, and one hot afternoon I found a coal-black butterfly which I took to be a small blue. It was afterwards identified as a chimney sweeper, a small and dingy moth which is, however, very like a butterfly in appearance.

This embankment was just the place where one might conceivably find a rare blue, for had not my parson friend, mentioned in an earlier chapter, taken a very rare 'blue' in such a locality some years before? He had been hunting along the banks of a single track line in Warwickshire and had taken what he thought was a common blue. When he examined it at leisure he found it was a Short Tailed or Bloxworth Blue, an exceedingly rare British butterfly which has only been taken on very few occasions.

One ramble stands out brilliantly in the memory. One hot June afternoon we had followed this railway along for some miles, and seeing a wood away to the right we set out to explore it. How hot it was walking across the endless fields, how grateful we were to reach the shade of the sweet woods! A little brook ran along the verge and finding a small sandy pool we stripped and lay in the water, allowing the bright ripples to purl over our bodies. Refreshed, we plunged into the trees, pushing our way between the hazel thickets. In a few moments my brother let out an excited shout. Round a hazel bush floated a white admiral, the first we had ever seen. We caught four that afternoon and later, in a gorgeous clearing pink with willow herb, we captured our first magnificent specimen of a silver-washed fritillary. Hitherto we had only seen these lovely insects in *The Butterflies of the British Isles*, a much-thumbed and tattered volume which we kept in the home-made book-case in our 'digs'.

We went many times again to 'our' wood, as we called it, and saw many more rare and beautiful butterflies. Red-backed shrikes were common in the tall unkempt hedges which bordered the little meadows; this was a species we never saw at home in the midlands.

The rarest bird I ever saw near Gordon Hill was a hobby, and not only did I see the bird but found the nest as well, which contained eggs. It was built in the old nest of a carrion crow, and I took an egg to the curator of the Natural History Museum in South Kensington, to make certain of its identity.

Canals and canal banks seem to attract birds even more than do railway embankments, especially where the canal runs through a cutting. Unlike the railway cuttings the banks are not tended with such care, and thorns and other bushes are allowed to grow. In time a steep canal bank may become quite impassable, for the thicket extends from the top to the very water's edge. Under the overhanging branches the fish are fond of lying in wait for numerous caterpillars and other bugs and beetles which fall off the leaves into the murky waters. Dog roses run riot all up the slope and in June these banks are a rare sight for the naturalist. The finches flock to the dense thickets; bullfinches, green-finches, chaffinches, pipits and yellow-hammers, nightingales and warblers, and always, where the sedges grow up into the overhanging branches, the sedge warblers sing continuously by day and night, vying with the nightingale. Their song is the very voice of summer; and as an accompaniment the warm water slaps a sleepy lullaby under the hanging dog rose. The exquisite pink buds, which alas! so soon lose that first flush, are reflected in the water; soon the boat-shaped petals will fall and be carried away by the passing wind.

The 'chug chugging' barges come round the bend of the canal, their stuttering engines audible from a great distance on a still evening. The bargee's wife leans her red and brawny arms across the painted tiller handle, the brass winks bright in the sun, the paintwork is spick and span. On the doors of the little cabin are painted gaudy castles; there is some superstition about this castle design, all the barges have it. Two dirty children play on the narrow decking and a dog is sitting in the bow staring down the shining path of the canal. The horse-drawn barge will soon be only a memory, which is a pity. After the barge has passed and the churned water has boiled to a calm, the big tench roll over among the weeds. The really hefty fellows only feed in the very hot weather; they are strong fighters and unless one's tackle is stout, will bury themselves in the weeds and break the cast. 'Tench weather' is like 'carp weather', those still hot days when the hay lies in the fields are the best times to catch them. It is a very handsome fish, both in colour and proportion; a fresh-caught specimen reminds me of an antique bronze.

The pike are fond of waiting in ambush under those over-hanging branches, their wicked shovel mouths and cruel eyes alert for the passing silver roach. Perch from these canals are much paler in colour than pond perch, some are almost dun coloured on the back, and the fins an anaemic pink instead of a hunting scarlet.

In the first warm days of spring when the sun shines on the water the pike begin to think of spawning. Walking along the tow path you will see a commotion among the water weeds, the handsome arrow heads shake and there is a flash of a copper side as a jack turns his barred flank. After their winter torpor the roach swim near the surface. Every-where there is a sense of awakening life. The croaking of frogs is incessant, the margins of the bank are a struggling mass. Though the tangled wall of hawthorn is yet bare, there is a promise of opening buds, soon a white wall of blossom will cover the cutting. Hawthorns thrive on a sheltered slope, they do not grow tall and raggedly; close-set and well-proportioned bushes clothe the whole of the gentle slopes.

In some parts of this midland county the canals are quite

beautiful, almost as beautiful as a river, though the water is always a khaki colour. Some years back the traffic on the canals languished and weeds began to choke these inland waterways. Now there has been a revival, no transport is so cheap and though it is slow it is sure.

The hedges bordering the canals are kept in order by the Canal Company (I am speaking of a certain canal I know well close to my home) and a special 'woodcutter's barge' is seen in the winter months. The men, whose job it is to keep the hedges trimmed and laid, live all the year round in this house-boat, and even in the depths of winter, when the canal is choked with ice and all traffic firmly locked, I see a blue thread of smoke coming from the cabin chimney as the woodmen cook their morning rasher.

It must be a dreary and lonely life, yet they seem to like it well enough, at any rate they are out in the open air.

The pike in these waterways never seem to attain any great size, though where there are 'basins' they will grow larger, fish of eight or nine pounds have been caught in such a basin close to my shoot.

Waterfowl are not particularly fond of canals, the constant passage of barges disturbs them and only the water-hens and dabchicks frequent the reedy margins.

Wild duck are too shy of the close proximity of banks and hedges and only drop in occasionally during the autumn. In September and early October wild duck frequent small ponds and ditches in the fields and appear in places where they are not seen for the rest of the year. This is partly due to the restless spirit of migration, later they will go away to the large sheets of water, sometimes in a distant county, the coast, or overseas.

The smart reed bunting is always found along the tow path, especially where there is any thick reed growth. The cock is a very lovely bird when in full breeding attire, with his starched white collar and jet-black head; they build in the low waterside bushes, among the tall grass and reeds, sometimes quite away from the canal, among the low thorn bushes. The nest is well hidden and the hen will invariably feign a broken wing if you put her off.

In the twilight the hedgepigs come to drink in the shallows where the sedges grow. I believe they also enter water to rid themselves of ticks and lice, though I doubt if they succeed. I once saw a hedgehog wade into a pond until only the tip of his nose was showing. As age advances they become very asthmatical, and I have often been startled in the twilight by a sudden piggy sneeze from the depths of a bush, and on investigating have found an old hedgehog. They are quaint little 'land urchins' and have most engaging ways. I once brought a hedgehog in from the garden and gave it some worms in a tin. Hedgehog and tin were left overnight in a small lobby in my house and we were awakened in the small hours by strange clanking sounds from below. I went down and saw the tin wedged firmly over the little beast's head; he was blindly barging about, knocking against the wall and running his head against the table and door. He had got his snout right into the tin in an endeavour to secure the few remaining worms and was unable to get the tin off again.

Though in places the canal can be attractive and even beautiful, it can never equal the stream, the natural meadow brook. I have written of the charm of the field pond and hedgerow; the stream is perhaps the most appealing of the three. Only the other day I made up my mind to follow such a meadow brook from its source.

I began my journey from where it passes under a main road. Years ago there was an old stone bridge at this spot, but as it was a dangerous corner for motors it was pulled down and a hideous concrete affair put in its place.

The old bridge was built of warm sandstone with a rounded coping, on which generations of love sick-rustics had scratched their names and scored their transfixed hearts; some of the lettering was quite beautiful. Ivy had covered the stonework and every April I used to look for the wren's nest close to the arch, a cosy little leaf house with its tiny round window set near the top. Many a weary tramp has camped under the wall and the marks of their fires made round black scars among the green stream-side grass. Countless blistered feet have been refreshed in the cold crinkling waters, many a torturing thirst has been quenched in the dusty summer weather. There is no cover now for the gentleman of the road and no rough-hewn wall to blind the prying eyes of passers by. The tar from the 'turnpike' has polluted the stream.

No more does a friendly flame kindle beside the stout hazel bush, for the thicket which used to grow close to the wall was cut down when the new bridge was built. I remember how, in spring, the lambs' tails used to hang over the water and sometimes a kingfisher perched on the hazel bough. The passing gust of a car or rumbling lorry was unknown in those far-off years.

The time I had chosen for my expedition was a late March day when the trees and hedges were yet bare and the catkins in their full glory. Many hazel bushes line this stream and when in full bloom the twigs are hidden in a tender green rain.

At first it winds through flat fields at the foot of a hill, its banks lined with bushes and bramble thickets. The twigs were still bare and the water could be seen gleaming through the tangled brakes. But every twig was dotted with whitish-green specks which in a few weeks would soon be leaves, and the branches had quite a bloom when the sun shone for a moment from a cloudy sky.

I revel in the sturdy health of bushes and trees, the bursting of the green fire imprisoned within each twig is a joy. In April all is so 'new minted'; every year I get the impression that never before have the leaves been so fresh a green or so luxuriantly thick. On all sides I saw this perfect health, this perpetual youth, even the old oaks gave promise of acres of green and luscious leaves.

In the fields, in the hedges, in woods and coppices, the fresh tide is rising, only men, beasts and birds gave evidence of decay. These fields and trees do not seem to know decay or death, can it be that they hold the secret of eternal life? It seems that the price we pay for movement and 'separateness' as it were, from the earth, is death. Yet I know that one day the trees must die, only the fields seem imperishable.

On looking about me I saw no decayed trees, all were healthy and soon to give glorious proof of life. One would have to search carefully to find a dead tree. The bushes appear to be akin to the fields, they know not death. They can be cut and cut again, but their life is deep within their roots, buried in the sandy bank of the stream. Every March new speckles will show on these purple-bloomed stems as the tide rises.

The greatest charm of this brook was the way it wound about. Here and there one could see traces of its old course; a fold in the ground or a moulded bank. In some places the water was shallow, brawling along over painted pebbles, hardly deep enough to wet the feet. And then at an angle I came to the first pool, which was quite deep under the far bank. Here the stream had eaten away the base of a steep sandy bluff so that there was a miniature cliff.

I was suddenly aware of scale. To the water vole, crossing the stream yonder (swept sideways by the current, his little

The Stream in Early Spring

eyes very bright) that bank must have seemed quite as high as the cliffs of Dover do to us. It took very little imagination to see the world through the eyes of the water vole. The tall elms opposite must have seemed like the Giant's Beanstalk, to go up and up into the very heaven.

The floods of winter had washed and washed at the sandy bank until the roots of the hawthorns on the bank above were coiled like serpents, bare to sun and wind. In time all the earth will be washed away and the trees will perish. But they will long outlast me, and I am jealous of the thorns when I know that they will be feeling the April sun and the March winds years hence when I shall have ceased to exist. A humbling thought which gave an added piquancy to my walk by the stream. At any rate I was all the more determined to explore its every bay, nothing should be hidden from me.

At the foot of the bluff was a perfect little beach of white sand, clean washed and printed with the claw marks of questing moorhens. On looking closely at the shadows between the exposed thorn roots I saw a collection of old leaves, November's leaves. They were blown there four months ago and the floods had not reached them.

I should not have been surprised if little elfin men do not live under those roots; I like to think they do. They are no bigger than my middle finger, so it is not surprising that no man has ever seen them, for they do not come out during the day, only in the dusk or very early morning and have a sixth sense which tells them of man's approach.

Like the trees and bushes they live for hundreds of years, perhaps indeed they never die. One day I will write of them, the story of the little men who are changeless and who have lived by this stream since it first began to flow. When the stream ceases to run they will go, like the old thorn bushes whose roots one winter's flood will wash away.

I once saw such a little man and I was (foolishly) afraid and cried. He was not a gnome from the stream or a woodland elf but a house elfin, as grey as his beard, grey all over, though his face was as wrinkled and red as an old hip berry. Children do see these things, but when they tell their parents and are answered by scornful incredulity and amusement they keep such matters to themselves. I am afraid no adult person has ever seen a fairy, unless they be undeveloped people, the Peter Pans of life. Having seen a fairy I believe in them, so I suppose I am undeveloped.

Surely these gnomes must have a busy time in the autumn; stick picking, acorn gathering, making crab-apple jelly which they sweeten with wild bees' honey, kippering stickle backs and minnows, in readiness for the long black winter nights when the snow flakes whirl and ice chokes the stream! What high revelry must be held then under those dark thorn roots! Perhaps those leaves, seemingly so carelessly blown under the shadow, are the remains of their winter fuel supply, for surely gnomes must have a fire to sit by in the winter, or do their mouse skins keep them warm? That they are hunters I have no doubt and eaters of meat.

I could see no fish up the brook, either in the pools or the shallows, yet if you were to come up this stream five weeks later you would see thousands, mostly minnows, stickle backs and dace. The latter haunt the deep holes, though they will feed at the tail of the pools on a fine summer's evening. Here and there are a few minute jack. I once found a jack of about an inch long in a semi-dry runlet which led from a ditch across a sheep track. The tiny fish was stranded and how it got there I cannot conceive. I took it home and put it in my rock pool where it still lives and grows.

After a mile or two had been followed, each foot of the stream being different from another, I came to an oak spinney through which it flowed. The rooks were busy around their nests, their spring caws rang on all sides, and green wood sorrel was breaking through the surface of the dried oak leaves. A kingfisher sped up the course of the brook piping shrilly, passing under the fallen willow which bridged the stream. They build up here and I have found the nest every year.

This old willow tree proved a useful bridge for rabbits, their droppings were all along the top of the horizontal trunk and here and there very bright green tufts of grass were growing from crevices in the bark. On the under side of the trunk, just above the water, was a large bracket fungus.

Already the willow wands were showing studs of silver and a cole tit swung among them, examining each bud. Back in the oak spinney a green woodpecker called continually; the spring weather excites them.

The time was now long past midday and I realized I could never hope to find the source of this magic brook. It seemed to run as strongly as ever and as deep. I had spent too long exploring every bend, every reach; I had only travelled a mile or two. The sun was hidden behind soft rain clouds and every blackbird and thrush within miles was singing. I could see the rooks dropping back to the oak tops and realized the fear the wild things have for man, the same fear which drives the little stream gnomes into hiding long before my footfall shakes the bank above.

The grass is so green in this meadow by the stream, the bright water furls and crinkles round the submerged root of the willow. For how many generations has this brook been flowing? The thought is staggering and sobering too.

This stream must be as old as the earth, yet it ripples as freshly as if it were born but yesterday. It is really only a few minutes ago that Cromwell's soldiers watered their horses here after the battle, but let us cease to think of things in terms of Time, to measure the vast earth by our little selves. Our own history is another tale, of no consequence. We have deliberately turned away from Nature and the peace and joy it offers us, yet it could so influence our pitifully brief span. Man has only blood and tears to offer, Nature has all that makes life worth living, yet we turn away as blind and deaf as stones.

Perched high on a willow twig a thrush was singing a refrain over and over again. To my ear it seemed to be saying 'eternity! eternity! eternity!'

And it is true what the thrush is singing. This wonder of life reborn is eternal for as long as the earth shall remain.

For myself I only want to live in this green hour, to feel the soft spring rain and see the brave resurrection of life, the life of the fields which knows no death or lasting destruction.

Finis

HAUNTED RIDE

There's a ride in the woods that the poacher shuns,
No wires are set in the rabbit runs,
And the dark firs sigh against the sky
When evening comes.

There's a ride in the woods where hounds won't follow,
They lose the scent in the Upper Hollow,
And horses shy when they pass by
That ride in the woods.

There's a ride in the woods where no keeper goes,
Where the proud cock pheasant seldom crows,
And what stalks there when the moon is bare
God only knows!

1939